sweet food

Kay Scarlett

LAUREL
GLEN

San Diego, California

Contents

Baked

Strawberry roulade

2 eggs
1 egg white
$\frac{1}{2}$ cup superfine sugar
$\frac{3}{4}$ cup self-rising flour
1 tablespoon superfine sugar, extra
1 cup smooth ricotta cheese
1 teaspoon vanilla extract
$\frac{1}{3}$ cup confectioners' sugar
$1\frac{2}{3}$ cups strawberries, hulled and
  chopped

Preheat the oven to 400°F. Lightly grease a $10\frac{1}{2}$ x 12 inch jelly-roll pan and line with waxed paper, allowing the paper to hang over the two long sides.

Using an electric mixer, beat the eggs, egg white, and sugar in a large bowl on high speed for 5 minutes or until light and foamy. Sift the flour into the bowl and fold in quickly and lightly.

Pour the mixture into the prepared pan and smooth the surface. Bake for 8–10 minutes or until the sponge cake springs back when lightly pressed. Lay a sheet of waxed paper on a clean dish towel and sprinkle lightly with the extra superfine sugar.

Unmold the sponge cake, place on the sugared paper, remove the waxed paper, and, starting from a short end, roll up the sponge cake with the paper, using the dish towel as a guide. Cool for 30 minutes.

Mix the ricotta cheese, vanilla, and confectioners' sugar together with a wooden spoon. Unroll the sponge cake and spread with the ricotta mixture, leaving a $\frac{3}{4}$ inch border at the far end. Sprinkle with the strawberries, then carefully reroll the sponge cake. Trim the ends, then cut into slices to serve.

Serves 8

Apricot and macaroon bars

⅓ cup unsalted butter, softened
⅓ cup superfine sugar
1 egg
1½ cups all-purpose flour
½ teaspoon baking powder

Filling
1⅓ cups dried apricots, roughly
   chopped
1 tablespoon Grand Marnier
2 tablespoons superfine sugar

Topping
⅓ cup unsalted butter
⅓ cup superfine sugar
1 teaspoon vanilla extract
2 eggs
3 cups dried shredded coconut
⅓ cup all-purpose flour
½ teaspoon baking powder

Preheat the oven to 350°F. Lightly grease an 8 x 12 inch baking pan and line with waxed paper. Cream the butter and sugar until light and fluffy. Add the egg and beat well. Sift the flour and baking powder and fold into the butter mixture with a metal spoon. Press firmly into the pan and bake for 20–25 minutes or until golden brown. Allow to cool.

To make the filling, combine the apricots, Grand Marnier, sugar, and ½ cup boiling water in a bowl. Set aside for 30 minutes, then purée in a food processor. Spread evenly over the cooled base.

To make the topping, cream the butter, sugar, and vanilla until light and fluffy. Gradually add the eggs, beating well after each addition. Fold in the coconut, flour, and baking powder with a large metal spoon. Spoon onto the apricot mixture, allowing it to remain lumpy and loose—do not press down. Bake for 20–25 minutes or until lightly golden.

Makes 16 pieces

Orange and almond cake

2 large navel oranges
6 eggs, separated
1 tablespoon orange blossom water
   or orange liqueur
1 cup superfine sugar
3 cups ground almonds
1 teaspoon baking powder
3 navel oranges, peeled, pith and
   membrane removed, thinly sliced,
   to garnish

Orange syrup
2 cups fresh orange juice, strained
$3/4$ cup superfine sugar
$1/4$ cup Sauternes

Grease and lightly flour a 9 inch springform cake pan, tipping out any excess flour. Put the whole oranges into a saucepan filled with water. Boil for 2 hours, topping up with water as needed. Remove the oranges, quarter them, and process in a food processor until smooth. Allow to cool. Preheat the oven to 350°F.

Place the egg yolks, orange blossom water, and superfine sugar in a large bowl and beat until smooth, then stir in the orange purée and mix well. Whisk the egg whites in a clean, dry bowl until firm peaks form. Add the ground almonds and baking powder to the orange mixture, stir well, then fold in the egg whites. Pour into the cake pan and bake for 1 hour or until firm—cover with aluminum foil if it overbrowns while baking. Cool in the pan, then transfer to a serving plate.

To make the syrup, put the orange juice, sugar, and Sauternes in a saucepan over medium heat and stir until the sugar is dissolved. Reduce the heat and simmer for 20 minutes or until reduced by half and slightly syrupy, skimming off any impurities.

Cut the cake into wedges, garnish with orange slices, and drizzle with syrup. Delicious served with whipped cream.

Serves 6–8

Spiced molasses gingerbread cookies

½ cup unsalted butter, cubed
   and softened
½ cup dark brown sugar
¼ cup molasses, preferably dark
1 egg
2 cups all-purpose flour
¼ cup self-rising flour
3 teaspoons ground ginger
2 teaspoons ground cinnamon
¾ teaspoon ground cloves
¾ teaspoon ground nutmeg
1 teaspoon baking soda

Tinted icing
1 egg white
½ teaspoon lemon juice
1 cup confectioners' sugar, sifted
assorted food colorings

Lightly grease two cookie sheets. Beat the butter and sugar until light and creamy, then beat in the molasses and egg. Fold in the combined sifted flours, spices, and baking soda. Turn out onto a lightly floured surface and knead until smooth. Cover with plastic wrap and chill for 10 minutes.

Divide the dough in half and roll out between two sheets of lightly floured waxed paper to a ¼ inch thickness. Lay the dough on the cookie sheets and chill for 15 minutes, until just firm. Preheat the oven to 350°F.

Cut out the dough using a 2¾ inch, heart-shaped cutter. Using a ½ inch plain cutter, cut a hole at the top of each heart. (You can thread these with ribbon to hang up the cookies.) Lay on the cookie sheets and bake for 10 minutes. Leave for 5 minutes, then cool on a wire rack.

To make the icing, whisk the egg white until foamy. Add the lemon juice and sugar and stir until glossy. Tint the icing with food coloring, then spoon into paper pastry bags, seal the end, and snip off the tips. Decorate the cookies with the icing.

Makes about 36

Flourless chocolate cake

1 lb. good-quality semisweet
chocolate, chopped
6 eggs
2 tablespoons Frangelico or brandy
1½ cups ground hazelnuts
1 cup whipping cream
confectioners' sugar, to dust
heavy cream, to serve

Preheat the oven to 300°F. Grease a deep, 8 inch round cake pan and line the bottom with waxed paper. Place the chocolate in a heatproof bowl. Half-fill a saucepan with water, boil, then remove from the heat and sit the bowl over the pan—don't let the bowl touch the water. Stir occasionally until the chocolate melts.

Put the eggs in a large, heatproof bowl and add the Frangelico. Put the bowl over a pan of barely simmering water—don't let it touch the water. Beat with an electric mixer on high speed for 7 minutes or until light and foamy. Remove from the heat.

Using a metal spoon, quickly and lightly fold the chocolate and ground nuts into the egg mixture until just combined. Fold in the whipped cream and pour into the cake pan. Put the cake pan in a shallow roasting pan. Pour hot water into the roasting pan to come halfway up the side of the cake pan. Bake for 1 hour or until just set. Remove the cake pan from the oven and cool to room temperature. Cover with plastic wrap and refrigerate overnight.

Invert the cake onto a plate, remove the paper, and cut into slices. Dust with confectioners' sugar and serve with whipped cream.

Serves 10

Sticky toffee bars

1 1/3 cups pitted dates,
  roughly chopped
1 teaspoon baking soda
1 cup unsalted butter
1 1/2 cups self-rising flour
1 teaspoon vanilla extract
1 teaspoon baking powder
3 eggs
1/3 cup milk
2 tablespoons light brown sugar
3/4 cup confectioners' sugar
3/4 cup chopped walnuts

Preheat the oven to 350°F. Lightly grease an 8 x 12 inch baking pan and line with waxed paper, allowing paper to hang over the two long sides.

Place the dates in a saucepan with 3/4 cup water, bring to a boil, then reduce the heat and simmer gently for 10 minutes—make sure the water doesn't evaporate completely. Add the baking soda and allow to cool.

Place 3/4 cup of the butter, the flour, vanilla extract, baking powder, eggs, and 1/3 cup of the milk in a food processor and mix in short bursts for 1 minute or until well blended. Add the dates and pulse to blend. Do not overprocess.

Place the mixture in the baking pan and bake for 20 minutes or until a skewer inserted in the center comes out clean. Set aside to cool.

Place the remaining butter and milk and the brown sugar in a saucepan and heat gently to dissolve the sugar. Add the confectioners' sugar and mix well. Spread over the top when cool and sprinkle with the walnuts.

Makes 18 pieces

Angel food cake with chocolate sauce

1 cup all-purpose flour
1 cup superfine sugar
10 egg whites, at room temperature
1 teaspoon cream of tartar
½ teaspoon vanilla extract

Chocolate sauce
9 oz. semisweet chocolate, chopped
¾ cup whipping cream
¼ cup unsalted butter, chopped

Preheat the oven to 350°F. Have an ungreased angel food cake pan ready. Sift the flour and ½ cup of the sugar four times into a large bowl. Set aside. Beat the egg whites, cream of tartar, and ¼ teaspoon salt in a clean, large bowl with an electric mixer until soft peaks form. Gradually add the remaining sugar and beat until thick and glossy.

Add the vanilla extract. Sift half the flour and sugar mixture over the meringue and gently fold into the mixture with a metal spoon. Repeat with the remaining flour and sugar. Spoon into the cake pan and bake for 45 minutes or until a skewer comes out clean when inserted into the center of the cake. Gently loosen around the side of the cake with a spatula, then unmold the cake and set on a wire rack to cool completely.

To make the sauce, put the chocolate, cream, and butter in a saucepan. Stir over low heat until the chocolate has melted and the mixture is smooth. Drizzle over the cake and serve.

Serves 8

Note: Ensure the angel food cake pan is very clean and not greased or the cake will not rise and will slip down the side of the pan.

Vanilla bars

1 lb. store-bought, unbaked
   puff pastry
1 cup superfine sugar
3/4 cup cornstarch
1/2 cup plain custard powder
4 cups whipping cream
1/4 cup unsalted butter, cubed
2 teaspoons vanilla extract
3 egg yolks

Icing
1 1/2 cups confectioners' sugar
1/4 cup passion fruit pulp
1 tablespoon unsalted butter, melted

Preheat the oven to 415°F. Lightly grease two cookie sheets with oil. Line the bottom and sides of a shallow, 9 inch square cake pan with aluminum foil, allowing the foil to hang over two opposite sides.

Divide the pastry in half, roll each piece into a 10 inch square, 1/8 inch thick, and put on a cookie sheet. Prick all over with a fork and bake for 8 minutes or until golden. Trim each pastry sheet to a 9 inch square. Put one sheet, top side down, in the cake pan.

Combine the sugar, cornstarch, and custard powder in a saucepan. Add the cream, stirring constantly over medium heat for 2 minutes or until it boils and thickens. Add the butter and vanilla and stir until smooth. Remove from the heat and whisk in the egg yolks until combined. Spread the custard over the pastry in the pan, then cover with the other pastry sheet, top side down. Allow to cool completely.

To make the icing, combine the confectioners' sugar, passion fruit pulp, and butter in a bowl and stir.

Remove from the pan using the aluminum foil as handles. Ice the top and allow to set before cutting with a serrated knife.

Makes 9 pieces

Sponge cake with fruit and cream

4 eggs
1 teaspoon vanilla extract
1/2 cup superfine sugar
1/2 cup self-rising flour
1/2 cup cornstarch
2 tablespoons raspberry preserves
1 1/4 cups heavy cream
confectioners' sugar, to dust
colored sugar sprinkles, to decorate

Preheat the oven to 350°F. Grease two shallow, 8 inch cake pans and line each bottom with waxed paper. Beat the eggs, vanilla, and sugar with an electric mixer for 5 minutes or until pale and creamy—the mixer should leave a trail in the mixture.

Sift the flours together on a sheet of waxed paper. Gently transfer the flour to the egg and sugar mixture and fold quickly and lightly using a large metal spoon—do not overmix or it will lose volume. Divide the mixture evenly between the pans. Bake for 20 minutes or until a skewer comes out clean when inserted into the center of each cake. Leave in the pans for 5 minutes, then unmold and set on a wire rack to cool completely.

Spread one cake with the raspberry preserves and whipped cream, then place the other cake on top. Dust with confectioners' sugar and, if desired, decorate with the sprinkles.

Serves 8

Fig and raspberry cake

3/4 cup unsalted butter
3/4 cup superfine sugar
1 egg
1 egg yolk
2 2/3 cups all-purpose flour
1 teaspoon baking powder
4 figs, quartered
grated zest of 1 orange
1 2/3 cups raspberries
2 tablespoons sugar

Preheat the oven to 350°F. Cream the butter and sugar in a bowl until light and pale. Add the eggs and beat again. Sift the flour over the bowl and fold in with the baking powder and a pinch of salt. Chill for 15 minutes, until firm enough to roll out.

Lightly grease a 9 inch springform pan. Divide the dough in two and roll out one piece large enough to fit the bottom of the pan. Cover with the figs, orange zest, and raspberries. Roll out the remaining dough and place it over the filling. Lightly brush the dough with water and sprinkle with sugar.

Bake for 30 minutes or until the top and bottom of the cake are cooked. Insert a skewer into the cake to see if it is ready—there should be no wet cake mixture clinging to the skewer. Serve with whipped cream or mascarpone.

Serves 6

Note: If fresh figs are not available, you can use the same amount of dried figs but you need to rehydrate them first. Simmer them in orange juice for 5 minutes, until they are plumped up and soft.

Chocolate caramel bars

7 oz. chocolate cookies, crushed
1/3 cup unsalted butter, melted
2 tablespoons dried shredded
coconut
1/2 cup unsalted butter, extra
14 oz. can sweetened condensed
milk
1/3 cup superfine sugar
3 tablespoons maple syrup
9 oz. semisweet chocolate
2 teaspoons oil

Grease a shallow, 12 x 8 inch baking pan and line with waxed paper, allowing paper to hang over the two long sides.

Combine the cookies, melted butter, and coconut in a bowl, then press into the pan and smooth the surface.

Combine the butter, condensed milk, sugar, and maple syrup in a small saucepan. Stir over low heat for 15 minutes or until the sugar has dissolved and the mixture is smooth, thick, and lightly colored. Remove from the heat and cool slightly. Pour over the cookie base and smooth the surface. Refrigerate for 30 minutes or until firm.

Chop the chocolate into small, evenly sized pieces and place in a heatproof bowl. Bring a saucepan of water to a boil and remove from the heat. Place the bowl over the saucepan, making sure the bowl doesn't touch the water. Stir occasionally until the chocolate has melted. Add the oil and stir until smooth. Spread the caramel on top and leave until partially set before marking into twenty-four triangles. Refrigerate until firm. Cut into triangles before serving.

Makes 24 triangles

Yogurt cake with syrup

3/4 cup unsalted butter, softened
1 cup superfine sugar
5 eggs, separated
1 cup plain yogurt
2 teaspoons grated lemon zest
1/2 teaspoon vanilla extract
2 1/4 cups all-purpose flour, sifted
2 teaspoons baking powder
1/2 teaspoon baking soda
heavy cream, to serve

Syrup
1 cup superfine sugar
1 cinnamon stick
1 1/2 inch strip lemon zest
1 tablespoon lemon juice

Preheat the oven to 350°F and lightly grease an 8 x 4 inch loaf pan.

Place the butter and sugar in a bowl and beat until light and creamy. Add the egg yolks gradually, beating well after each addition. Stir in the yogurt, lemon zest, and vanilla. Fold in the flour, baking powder, and baking soda with a metal spoon.

Whisk the egg whites in a clean, dry bowl until stiff and fold into the mixture. Spoon into the prepared pan and bake for 50 minutes or until a skewer comes out clean when inserted into the center of the cake. Cool in the pan for 10 minutes, then unmold and set on a wire rack to cool.

Meanwhile, to make the syrup, place the sugar and cinnamon stick in a small saucepan with 3/4 cup cold water. Stir over medium heat until the sugar is dissolved. Bring to a boil, add the lemon zest and juice, then reduce the heat and simmer for 5–6 minutes. Strain.

Pour the syrup over the cake and wait for most of it to be absorbed before serving. Cut into slices and serve warm with whipped cream.

Serves 8–10

Raspberry and coconut bars

2¼ cups all-purpose flour
3 tablespoons ground almonds
2 cups superfine sugar
1 cup unsalted butter, chilled
½ teaspoon ground nutmeg
½ teaspoon baking powder
4 eggs
1 teaspoon vanilla extract
1 tablespoon lemon juice
2½ cups fresh or thawed frozen
  raspberries
1 cup dried shredded coconut
confectioners' sugar, to dust

Preheat the oven to 350°F. Lightly grease a shallow, 8 x 12 inch pan and line with waxed paper, allowing the paper to hang over the two long sides.

Sift 1¾ cups of the flour into a bowl. Add the ground almonds and ½ cup of the superfine sugar and stir to combine. Cut the butter into the flour with a pastry blender or rub in with your fingertips until it resembles fine bread crumbs. Press the mixture into the pan and bake for 20–25 minutes or until golden. Reduce the oven temperature to 300°F.

Sift the nutmeg, baking powder, and the remaining flour onto a piece of waxed paper. Beat the eggs, vanilla, and remaining sugar with an electric mixer for 4 minutes or until light and fluffy. Fold in the flour with a large metal spoon. Stir in the lemon juice, raspberries, and coconut and pour over the base.

Bake for 1 hour or until golden and firm. Chill in the pan, then cut into pieces. Dust with confectioners' sugar.

Makes 30 pieces

Macadamia and white chocolate cookies

1 1/3 cups macadamia nuts, lightly
toasted (see page 390)
1 egg
3/4 cup light brown sugar
2 tablespoons sugar
1 teaspoon vanilla extract
1/2 cup vegetable oil
1/2 cup all-purpose flour
1/4 cup self-rising flour
1/4 teaspoon ground cinnamon
1/2 cup dried shredded coconut
3/4 cup white chocolate chips

Roughly chop the toasted macadamia
nuts and set them aside.

Using an electric mixer, beat the egg
and sugars in a bowl until light and
fluffy. Add the vanilla and oil. Using a
wooden spoon, stir in the sifted flours,
cinnamon, coconut, macadamia
nuts, and chocolate and mix well.
Refrigerate for 30 minutes. Preheat
the oven to 350°F. Grease and line
two cookie sheets.

Form rounded tablespoons of the
mixture into balls and place on the
cookie sheets, pressing the mixture
together with your fingertips if it is
crumbly. Bake for 12–15 minutes or
until golden. Cool slightly on the
sheets, then transfer to a wire rack.

Makes about 25

Variation: Semisweet chocolate
chips can be used instead of
white chocolate chips.

Date chocolate torte

3/4 cup slivered almonds
4 oz. semisweet chocolate, coarsely
  chopped
2/3 cup dried dates, pitted
3 egg whites
1/2 cup superfine sugar
1/2 cup heavy cream
2 teaspoons superfine sugar, extra
1 oz. semisweet chocolate, grated,
  extra

Preheat the oven to 350°F. Grease an 8 1/2 inch round springform pan and line with aluminum foil. Finely chop the almonds and chocolate in a food processor, and chop the dates with a sharp knife.

Beat the egg whites with an electric mixer until soft peaks form. Slowly add the sugar and continue beating until it dissolves. Fold in the almond and chocolate mixture, then the dates. Spoon the mixture into the prepared pan and level the surface. Bake for 30–35 minutes or until set and it starts to come away from the sides. Cool in the pan before carefully unmolding and setting on a serving plate.

To serve, whip the cream and extra sugar until soft peaks form. Spread the cream evenly over the top with a spatula. Sprinkle with the grated chocolate to decorate.

Serves 6

Note: This is great with coffee for a special occasion or dessert.
Storage: Without cream, this torte keeps well for 5–6 days. With cream, it is best eaten on the day of baking.

Pecan brownies

4 oz. semisweet chocolate
1/3 cup unsalted butter, softened
1 cup superfine sugar
1 teaspoon vanilla extract
2 eggs
2/3 cup all-purpose flour
1/4 cup cocoa powder
1/2 teaspoon baking powder
1 cup roughly chopped pecans

Preheat the oven to 350°F. Grease a 6 1/2 inch square pan and line the bottom with waxed paper, allowing the paper to hang over two opposite sides.

Chop the chocolate into small, evenly sized pieces and place in a heatproof bowl. Bring a saucepan of water to a boil and remove from the heat. Position the bowl over the saucepan, making sure the bowl doesn't touch the water. Allow to rest, stirring occasionally, until melted. Cool slightly.

Beat the butter, sugar, and vanilla with an electric mixer until thick and creamy. Beat in the eggs one at a time, beating well after each addition. Stir in the chocolate.

Sift and combine the flour, cocoa, and baking powder and add to the mixture, then fold in the pecans with a metal spoon. Spoon into the pan and smooth the surface. Bake for 30–35 minutes or until firm and it comes away from the sides of the pan. Cool in the pan, remove, and cut into squares.

Makes 16 pieces

Zucchini and walnut cake

2½ cups walnuts
4 cups grated zucchini
1 cup canola oil
1½ cups raw sugar
3 eggs
2½ cups self-rising flour, sifted
1½ teaspoons ground cinnamon
1 teaspoon ground nutmeg

Preheat the oven to 325°F. Grease a 9 x 5 inch loaf pan and line the base and two long sides with a sheet of waxed paper.

Roughly chop 1¾ cups of the walnuts. Put the grated zucchini in a large bowl with the oil, sugar, eggs, and chopped walnuts and mix well. Stir in the flour, cinnamon, and nutmeg.

Spoon the mixture into the pan and arrange the remaining walnuts on top. Bake for 1 hour 10 minutes or until a skewer comes out clean when inserted into the center of the cake. Leave in the pan for 20 minutes before unmolding and setting on a wire rack to cool. Cut into slices and serve.

Serves 6–8

Storage: Wrap in aluminum foil when cooled. The cake will keep for 4–5 days.

Coconut and pineapple bars

1/3 cup dried shredded coconut
3/4 cup self-rising flour
1/2 cup all-purpose flour
3/4 cup light brown sugar
2 tablespoons sunflower seeds
2 tablespoons sesame seeds
1/2 cup chopped macadamia nuts
1/3 cup chopped dates
1 tablespoon chopped candied ginger
1/2 cup dried shredded coconut
8 oz. can crushed pineapple, drained
1/3 cup unsalted butter, melted
2 eggs, lightly beaten

Icing
2 cups confectioners' sugar
2 tablespoons unsalted butter, melted
1 1/2 tablespoons lemon juice

Preheat the oven to 325°F. Spread 1/3 cup shredded coconut evenly on a cookie sheet and toast for 5–8 minutes or until lightly golden. Grease a shallow, 8 x 12 inch baking pan and line with enough waxed paper to overlap the longer sides; this will make the bars easier to remove.

Sift the self-rising and all-purpose flours into a large bowl. Add the brown sugar, seeds, macadamia nuts, dates, ginger, and 1/2 cup coconut. Stir in the pineapple, melted butter, and beaten eggs and mix well.

Spoon the mixture into the prepared pan. Bake for 25–30 minutes or until golden brown. Cool in the pan, remove, and cover with the icing.

To make the icing, combine the confectioners' sugar, melted butter, and lemon juice in a small bowl. Stir in 1–2 teaspoons of boiling water to reach a smooth consistency. Spread evenly over the top. Sprinkle the top with the toasted shredded coconut and slice and serve when set.

Makes 24 pieces

Note: Use other nuts or seeds, such as pumpkin seeds or almonds, if desired.

Hawaiian macadamia cake

3 cups self-rising flour
1 teaspoon ground cinnamon
1½ cups superfine sugar
1 cup dried shredded coconut
5 eggs, lightly beaten
14 oz. can crushed pineapple in syrup
1½ cups vegetable oil
⅔ cup macadamia nuts, chopped

Lemon cream-cheese icing
¼ cup cream cheese, softened
2 tablespoons unsalted butter,
  softened
1 tablespoon lemon juice
1½ cups confectioners' sugar, sifted

Preheat the oven to 350°F. Grease a deep, 9 inch round cake pan. Line the bottom and side with two sheets of waxed paper, cutting the paper to extend an inch above the side of the pan.

Sift the flour and cinnamon into a large bowl, add the sugar and coconut, and stir to combine. Add the eggs, pineapple, and oil and mix well. Stir in the macadamia nuts.

Spoon the mixture into the prepared pan and level the surface. Bake for 1 hour 15 minutes or until a skewer comes out clean when inserted into the center of the cake—cover with aluminum foil if it looks as if it may brown before it's done. Leave in the pan for 30 minutes before unmolding and setting on a wire rack.

To make the lemon cream-cheese icing, beat the cream cheese and butter in a small bowl. Add the lemon juice and confectioners' sugar and beat until smooth. Spread over the cooled cake.

Serves 10–12

Madeira cake

3/4 cup unsalted butter, softened
3/4 cup superfine sugar
3 eggs, beaten
1 1/3 cups self-rising flour, sifted
2 teaspoons finely grated lemon zest
1 teaspoon lemon juice
2 teaspoons superfine sugar, extra,
   to sprinkle
confectioners' sugar, to dust
lemon zest, extra, to garnish

Preheat the oven to 315°F. Grease and flour a deep, 7 inch round cake pan, shaking out any excess.

Beat the butter and sugar with an electric mixer until pale and creamy. Add the eggs gradually, beating well after each addition. Fold in the flour, lemon zest, and juice until combined. When smooth, spoon into the prepared pan and level the surface. Sprinkle the extra superfine sugar on top.

Bake for 1 hour or until a skewer comes out clean when inserted into the center of the cake. Allow to cool for 15 minutes in the pan before unmolding and setting on a wire rack. To serve, dust with confectioners' sugar and garnish with lemon zest.

Serves 6

Storage: Wrapped in aluminum foil, the cake will keep for 4 days.

Ginger cheesecake bars

7 oz. ginger cookies, finely crushed
¼ cup unsalted butter, melted
½ teaspoon ground cinnamon
2 cups cream cheese
½ cup golden syrup or dark corn
  syrup
2 tablespoons superfine sugar
2 eggs
¼ cup finely chopped crystallized
  ginger
½ cup heavy cream, lightly whipped
½ cup heavy cream, extra
2 teaspoons superfine sugar, extra
¼ cup crystallized ginger, extra,
  thinly sliced

Preheat the oven to 325°F. Lightly grease an 8 x 12 inch baking pan and line with waxed paper, allowing the paper to hang over the two long sides.

Combine the cookies, butter, and cinnamon and press into the bottom of the pan. Refrigerate for 30 minutes or until firm.

Beat the cream cheese, golden syrup, and sugar with an electric mixer until light and fluffy. Add the eggs, one at a time, beating well after each addition. Fold in the ginger and lightly whipped cream. Spread over the base and bake for 25 minutes or until just set. Turn off the oven and cool with the door slightly ajar.

Remove the cheesecake from the pan and trim the edges. Beat the extra cream and sugar until soft peaks form, then spread over the cheesecake. Using a hot, dry knife, cut into three strips lengthwise and then cut each strip into eight pieces. Decorate with the extra ginger.

Makes 24 pieces

White chocolate chip cupcakes

½ cup unsalted butter, softened
¾ cup superfine sugar
2 eggs, lightly beaten
1 teaspoon vanilla extract
2 cups self-rising flour, sifted
½ cup buttermilk
1⅔ cups white chocolate chips
white chocolate, shaved, to decorate

White chocolate cream-cheese icing
3½ oz. white chocolate
¼ cup whipping cream
¾ cup cream cheese, softened
⅓ cup confectioners' sugar

Preheat the oven to 325°F. Lightly grease twelve standard (½ cup) muffin cups.

Beat the butter and sugar in a large bowl with an electric mixer until pale and creamy. Gradually add the eggs, beating well after each addition. Add the vanilla extract and beat until combined. Fold in the flour alternately with the buttermilk, then fold in the white chocolate chips.

Fill each muffin cup three-quarters full with the mixture and bake for 20 minutes or until a skewer comes out clean when inserted into the center of each cupcake. Leave in the muffin pan for 5 minutes before unmolding and setting out on a wire rack to cool—loosen around the edges if the muffins stick to the pan.

To make the icing, mix the chocolate and cream in a small saucepan over low heat until smooth. Cool slightly, then add to the cream cheese and confectioners' sugar and beat until the chocolate is melted and the mixture is smooth. Spread the icing over the cakes and garnish with white chocolate shavings.

Makes 12

Date caramel shortcake

½ cup unsalted butter, softened
½ cup superfine sugar
1 teaspoon vanilla extract
1 egg
2 cups all-purpose flour
1 teaspoon baking powder
1 cup roughly chopped seedless
  dates
1 tablespoon light brown sugar
2 teaspoons cocoa powder
½ tablespoon unsalted butter, extra
confectioners' sugar, to sprinkle

Preheat the oven to 350°F. Lightly grease a shallow, 7 x 11 inch baking pan. Line with waxed paper, allowing the paper to hang over the two long sides.

Beat the butter, sugar, and vanilla with an electric mixer until light and fluffy. Beat in the egg, then transfer to a bowl. Fold in the combined sifted flour and baking powder in batches with a metal spoon.

Press half the dough into the pan. Form the other half into a ball, cover, and refrigerate for 30 minutes.

Place the dates, brown sugar, cocoa, extra butter, and 1 cup water in a small saucepan. Bring to a boil, stirring, then reduce the heat and simmer, stirring, for 12–15 minutes or until the dates are soft and the water has been absorbed. Spread onto a plate and refrigerate to cool quickly.

Spread the filling over the pastry base with a metal spatula, then grate the remaining dough over the top. Bake for 35 minutes or until light brown and crisp. Cool in the pan for 15 minutes, then lift onto a wire rack. Sprinkle with confectioners' sugar and cut into squares.

Makes 12 pieces

Crackle cookies

½ cup unsalted butter, cubed and
 softened
2 cups light brown sugar
1 teaspoon vanilla extract
2 eggs
2 oz. semisweet chocolate, melted
⅓ cup milk
2¾ cups all-purpose flour
2 tablespoons cocoa powder
2 teaspoons baking powder
¼ teaspoon ground allspice
⅔ cup chopped pecans
confectioners' sugar, to coat

Lightly grease two cookie sheets.
Beat the butter, sugar, and vanilla until
light and creamy. Beat in the eggs,
one at a time. Stir the chocolate and
milk into the butter mixture.

Sift the flour, cocoa, baking powder,
allspice, and a pinch of salt into the
butter mixture and mix well. Stir in
the pecans. Refrigerate for at least
3 hours or overnight.

Preheat the oven to 350°F. Roll
tablespoons of the mixture into balls
and roll each in the confectioners'
sugar to coat.

Place well apart on the cookie sheets.
Bake for 20–25 minutes or until lightly
browned. Leave for 3–4 minutes, then
cool on a wire rack.

Makes about 60

Chocolate banana cake

3 ripe bananas, mashed (about 1 cup)
3/4 cup superfine sugar
1 1/2 cups self-rising flour
2 eggs, lightly beaten
3 tablespoons light olive oil
1/4 cup milk
3 1/2 oz. semisweet chocolate, grated
3/4 cup walnuts, chopped

Preheat the oven to 350°F. Grease an 8 x 4 inch loaf pan and line the bottom with waxed paper.

Mix the mashed bananas and sugar in a large bowl until just combined. Add the sifted flour, eggs, oil, and milk. Stir the mixture gently for 30 seconds with a wooden spoon. Fold in the chocolate and walnuts.

Pour the mixture into the pan and bake for 55 minutes or until a skewer comes out clean when inserted into the center of the cake. Allow to cool in the pan for 5 minutes before turning onto a wire rack. If desired, serve warm with whipped cream.

Serves 6–8

Note: In warm weather, chocolate can be grated more easily if it is left to harden in the freezer for a few minutes beforehand.

Fig and cinnamon bars

½ cup unsalted butter, softened
¼ cup light brown sugar,
  firmly packed
1 teaspoon ground cinnamon
1½ cups all-purpose flour
2⅓ cups dried figs
1 cinnamon stick
½ cup superfine sugar

Preheat the oven to 350°F. Lightly grease a 7 x 11 inch baking pan and line with waxed paper, allowing paper to hang over the two long sides.

Beat the butter, brown sugar, and cinnamon until light and fluffy, then fold in the flour with a large metal spoon. Press the mixture evenly into the pan and bake for 25 minutes. Cool slightly.

Place the dried figs, cinnamon stick, sugar, and 1½ cups boiling water in a saucepan, mix together, and bring to a boil. Reduce the heat and simmer for 20 minutes or until the figs have softened and the water has reduced by a third. Remove the cinnamon stick and place the mixture in a food processor. Process in short bursts until smooth.

Pour onto the cooked base and bake for 10 minutes or until set. Cool in the pan, then lift out and cut into squares.

Makes 15 squares

Lemon stars

½ cup unsalted butter, cubed and
  softened
½ cup superfine sugar
2 egg yolks
2 teaspoons finely grated lemon zest
1 ¼ cups all-purpose flour
¾ cup coarse cornmeal
confectioners' sugar, to dust

Preheat the oven to 315°F. Line a
cookie sheet with waxed paper. Beat
the butter and sugar until creamy.
Mix in the egg yolks, lemon zest,
flour, and cornmeal until they form a
ball of soft dough. Roll out on a lightly
floured surface to ½ inch thick.

Cut out stars from the dough using
a 1 ¼ inch, star-shaped cutter. Place
on the cookie sheet and bake for
15–20 minutes or until lightly golden.
Cool on a wire rack and dust with the
confectioners' sugar.

Makes about 22

Pineapple pecan cake

$\frac{1}{3}$ cup unsalted butter, softened
1 cup sugar
2 eggs, lightly beaten
1$\frac{1}{2}$ cups all-purpose flour
1$\frac{3}{4}$ teaspoons baking powder
$\frac{1}{3}$ cup finely chopped pecans, toasted
$\frac{3}{4}$ cup finely chopped candied pineapple
$\frac{2}{3}$ cup milk

Preheat the oven to 350°F. Grease a 9 inch round cake pan and line the bottom with waxed paper. Beat the butter and sugar with an electric mixer until combined. Add the egg and beat until pale and creamy.

Sift together the flour, baking powder, and $\frac{1}{4}$ teaspoon salt. Add to the butter mixture with the pecans, pineapple, and milk, then beat on low for 1 minute or until almost smooth.

Spoon the mixture evenly into the prepared pan and smooth the surface. Bake for 1 hour or until a skewer comes out clean when inserted into the center of the cake. Leave in the pan for 10 minutes before turning onto a wire rack to cool. If desired, dust with confectioners' sugar just before serving.

Serves 8–10

Shredded pastries with almonds

1 cup unsalted butter, melted
1 cup ground pistachios
2 cups ground almonds
2½ cups superfine sugar
1 teaspoon ground cinnamon
¼ teaspoon ground cloves
1 tablespoon brandy
1 egg white, lightly beaten
1 lb. kataifi pastry (Greek shredded
   pastry) or shredded phyllo dough,
   left at room temperature for 2 hours
   (without unwrapping)
1 teaspoon lemon juice
2 inch strip lemon zest
4 cloves
1 cinnamon stick
1 tablespoon honey

Preheat the oven to 325°F. Brush an 8 x 12 inch cookie sheet with some melted butter. Put the nuts in a bowl with ½ cup of the superfine sugar, cinnamon, cloves, and brandy. Add the beaten egg white and stir to make a paste. Divide the mixture into eight portions—form each into a "sausage" about 7 inches long.

Take a small handful of the pastry strands and spread them out fairly compactly with the strands running lengthwise toward you. The pastry should measure 10 x 7 inches. Brush with melted butter. Put one of the nut sausages along the end of the pastry nearest to you and roll up into a neat sausage shape. Repeat with the other pastry portions. Place the rolls close together on the baking sheet and brush with melted butter. Bake for 50 minutes or until golden brown.

Place the remaining sugar in a small saucepan with 2 cups water and stir over low heat until dissolved. Add the lemon juice, zest, cloves, and cinnamon and boil for 10 minutes. Stir in the honey, then set aside until cool. When the pastries come out of the oven, pour the cold syrup over the top. Allow to cool completely before cutting each roll into five pieces.

Makes 40 pieces

Pecan and orange loaf cake

3/4 cup superfine sugar
2/3 cup unsalted butter, softened
2 eggs, lightly beaten
3/4 cup ground pecans
1 tablespoon grated orange zest
1 1/2 cups self-rising flour
1/2 cup milk
1 cup confectioners' sugar

Preheat the oven to 350°F. Grease a 9 x 5 inch loaf pan and line the bottom and the two long sides of the pan with waxed paper.

Beat the sugar and 1/2 cup of the butter with an electric mixer until pale and creamy. Gradually add the eggs, beating well after each addition. Add the pecans and 3 teaspoons of the orange zest, then gently fold in the sifted flour with a metal spoon alternately with the milk. Spoon the mixture into the prepared pan and smooth the surface.

Bake for 50–60 minutes or until a skewer comes out clean when inserted into the center of the cake. Leave in the pan for 10 minutes before unmolding and setting on a wire rack to cool.

To make the icing, place the confectioners' sugar, the remaining orange zest, and 1–2 tablespoons hot water in a bowl and mix until smooth and combined. Spread the icing over the cooled cake with a flat-bladed knife.

Serves 8–10

Poppy seed bars

1 cup all-purpose flour
1/3 cup unsalted butter, chilled and chopped
1/4 cup superfine sugar
1 egg yolk
1/4 cup poppy seeds
2 tablespoons milk, warmed
1/2 cup unsalted butter, extra
1/3 cup superfine sugar, extra
1 teaspoon finely grated lemon zest
1 egg
3/4 cup all-purpose flour, extra, sifted
1 cup confectioners' sugar
1/2 teaspoon finely grated lemon zest, extra
1 tablespoon lemon juice

Preheat the oven to 350°F. Grease a 14 x 4 1/2 inch, loose-bottomed tart pan. Sift the flour into a bowl and cut in the butter with a pastry blender or rub in with your fingers until it resembles bread crumbs. Stir in the sugar. Make a well in the center and add 2–3 teaspoons water and the egg yolk. Mix with a flat-bladed knife, using a cutting action until it comes together in beads. Press into a ball and flatten slightly. Cover in plastic wrap and chill for 15 minutes.

Roll out the dough to fit the bottom and sides of the pan. Trim the edges. Blind bake the pastry for 10 minutes (see page 392), then remove the paper and beads and bake for 5 minutes or until the pastry is dry. Cool.

Soak the poppy seeds in the milk for 10 minutes. Beat the extra butter and sugar and the zest until light and fluffy. Beat in the egg and stir in the poppy seed mixture and extra flour. Spread over the pastry and bake for 25 minutes or until light brown and cooked through. Cool in the pan until just warm.

Combine the confectioners' sugar, extra zest, and enough juice to form a paste. Spread over the top and cool.

Makes 14 pieces

Beer cake

1 cup all-purpose flour
1/2 teaspoon ground cinnamon
3 cups superfine sugar
1 cup plus 1 tablespoon unsalted
    butter, chopped
3 eggs
4 cups self-rising flour
1 cup golden raisins
2 cups beer
heavy cream, to serve

Preheat the oven to 350°F. Grease a deep, 10 inch round cake pan and line the bottom with waxed paper. To make the topping, mix together the all-purpose flour, cinnamon, and 1 cup of the sugar. Place in a food processor with 1/2 cup of the butter and combine.

Place the remaining butter in a large bowl with the remaining sugar and beat with an electric mixer until pale and creamy. Gradually add the eggs, beating well after each addition—the mixture may look curdled, but once you add the flour, it will come back together. Fold in the sifted flour, golden raisins, and beer.

Pour the mixture into the prepared pan and gather the topping together in your hands to form small balls, then sprinkle over the cake. Bake for 1 hour 50 minutes or until a skewer comes out clean when inserted into the center. Allow to cool in the pan before inverting onto a wire rack. If desired, serve with cream.

Serves 12

Butterfly cupcakes

½ cup unsalted butter, softened
¾ cup superfine sugar
1½ cups self-rising flour
½ cup milk
2 eggs
½ cup cream, softly whipped
1½ tablespoons strawberry preserves
confectioners' sugar, to dust

Preheat the oven to 350°F. Line a standard twelve-cup muffin pan with paper liners.

Beat the butter, sugar, flour, milk, and eggs with an electric mixer on low speed. Increase the speed and beat until smooth and pale. Divide evenly among the liners and bake for 30 minutes or until cooked and golden. Transfer to a wire rack to cool.

Cut shallow rounds from the center of each cake using the point of a sharp knife, then cut in half. Spoon 2 teaspoons cream into each cavity, top with 1 teaspoon preserves, and position two halves of the cake tops in the preserves to resemble butterfly wings. Dust with confectioners' sugar.

Makes 12

Note: If using foil liners instead of the standard paper liners as suggested, the size and number of butterfly cupcakes may vary.

Strawberry and mascarpone bars

3/4 cup unsalted butter, softened
1/3 cup superfine sugar
1 egg yolk
2 cups all-purpose flour, sifted
1 1/3 cups mascarpone
1/2 cup confectioners' sugar, sifted
1 tablespoon lemon juice
2 cups strawberries, cut into quarters
2 oz. semisweet chocolate

Preheat the oven to 350°F. Lightly grease a shallow, 12 x 8 inch baking pan and line with waxed paper, allowing the paper to hang over the two long sides.

Beat the butter and sugar with an electric mixer until light and fluffy. Add the egg yolk and beat well. Fold in the sifted flour until well combined. Press firmly into the prepared baking pan and prick all over with a fork. Bake for 25 minutes or until light brown. Cool completely.

Beat the mascarpone, confectioners' sugar, and juice with a wooden spoon until smooth. Stir in the strawberries. Spoon over the base and refrigerate for 3 hours or until firm.

Chop the chocolate into small, evenly sized pieces and place in a heatproof bowl. Bring a saucepan of water to a boil, then remove from the heat. Position the bowl over the saucepan, ensuring the bowl doesn't touch the water. Stand, stirring occasionally, until the chocolate has melted. Drizzle over the top, then cut into pieces.

Makes 24 pieces

Chocolate, ginger, and fig cake

½ cup unsalted butter, softened
1 cup firmly packed light brown sugar
2 eggs, lightly beaten
1½ cups self-rising flour
⅓ cup cocoa powder
¾ cup milk
⅔ cup dried figs, chopped
⅓ cup candied ginger, chopped

Preheat the oven to 350°F. Grease a 9 x 5 inch loaf pan and line the bottom with waxed paper. Beat the butter and sugar with an electric mixer until pale and creamy.

Gradually add the egg, beating well after each addition. Stir in the sifted flour and cocoa alternately with the milk to make a smooth batter. Fold in the figs and half the ginger.

Spoon the mixture into the prepared pan and smooth the surface. Sprinkle the remaining ginger on top. Bake for 1 hour or until a skewer comes out clean when inserted into the center of the cake. Allow the cake to cool in the pan for 5 minutes before inverting onto a wire rack.

Serves 8

Madeleines

3 eggs
1/2 cup superfine sugar
1 1/4 cups all-purpose flour
1/3 cup unsalted butter, melted
grated zest of 1 lemon and 1 orange

Preheat the oven to 400°F. Brush fourteen (or thirty small) madeleine molds with melted butter and coat with flour, then tap the pans to remove the excess flour.

Whisk the eggs and sugar until the mixture is thick and pale and the whisk leaves a trail when lifted. Gently fold in the flour, then the melted butter and lemon and orange zest. Spoon into the molds, leaving a little room for rising. Bake for 12 minutes (small madeleines will only need 7 minutes) or until very lightly golden and springy to the touch. Remove from the molds and cool on a wire rack.

Makes 14 (or 30 small)

Chocolate mud cake

1 cup all-purpose flour
1 cup self-rising flour
1/2 cup dark cocoa powder
1/2 teaspoon baking soda
2 3/4 cups sugar
1 lb. semisweet chocolate, chopped
1 3/4 cups unsalted butter
1/2 cup buttermilk
2 tablespoons vegetable oil
2 tablespoons instant espresso coffee
  granules or powder
4 eggs

Preheat the oven to 315°F. Brush a deep, 9 inch square cake pan with melted butter or oil. Line the bottom and sides with waxed paper so that the paper extends at least 3/4 inch above the rim.

Sift the flours, cocoa, and baking soda into a large bowl. Stir in the sugar and make a well in the center. Put 9 oz. of the chocolate and 1 cup of the butter in a saucepan. Add 3/4 cup of water and stir over low heat until melted. Gradually stir the chocolate mixture into the dry ingredients using a large metal spoon.

Whisk together the buttermilk, oil, coffee, and eggs in a large bowl and add to the mixture, stirring until smooth. Pour into the pan and bake for 1 hour 40 minutes or until a skewer comes out clean when inserted in the center. Cool in the pan, then turn out.

Combine the remaining chocolate and butter in a small saucepan and stir over low heat until smooth. Cool to room temperature, stirring often, until thick enough to spread. Turn the cake upside down, so that the uneven top becomes the bottom, and spread the icing over the entire cake. Allow the icing to set slightly before serving.

Serves 12

Lemon meringue muffins

1³/₄ cups self-rising flour
³/₄ cup superfine sugar
1 egg
1 egg yolk, extra
²/₃ cup milk
¹/₂ teaspoon vanilla extract
¹/₃ cup unsalted butter, melted
  and cooled
²/₃ cup lemon curd
2 egg whites
1 teaspoon superfine sugar, extra

Preheat the oven to 400°F. Grease twelve standard muffin cups. Sift the flour into a large bowl and stir in ¹/₄ cup of the superfine sugar. Make a well in the center. Put a pinch of salt, the egg, and egg yolk in a bowl and beat together. Stir in the milk, vanilla, and butter. Pour the egg mixture into the well. Fold until just combined—the batter will be lumpy.

Divide the muffin mixture among the cups. Bake for 15 minutes—the muffins will only rise a little. (Leave the oven on.) Cool the muffins in the pan for 10 minutes, then loosen with a knife but leave in the pan. Hollow out the center of each muffin with a melon baller. Fill a pastry bag with the lemon curd and fill the center of each muffin.

Whisk the egg whites in a clean, dry bowl until firm peaks form. Add a quarter of the remaining sugar at a time, beating well after each addition until firm peaks form. Put a heaping tablespoon of meringue on top of each muffin and form peaks with the back of a spoon. Sprinkle with a little superfine sugar and bake for 5 minutes or until the meringue is golden and crisp. Cool in the pan for 10 minutes, then carefully transfer to a wire rack. Serve warm or at room temperature.

Makes 12 regular muffins

Chocolate truffle macaroon bars

3 egg whites
$3/4$ cup superfine sugar
2 cups dried shredded coconut
9 oz. semisweet chocolate
$1\frac{1}{4}$ cups heavy cream
1 tablespoon cocoa powder

Preheat the oven to 350°F. Lightly grease a shallow, 12 x 8 inch baking pan and line with waxed paper, allowing paper to hang over the two long sides.

Beat the egg whites in a clean, dry bowl until soft peaks form. Slowly add the sugar, beating well after each addition until stiff and glossy. Fold in the coconut. Spread into the pan and bake for 20 minutes or until light brown. While still warm, press down lightly but firmly with a flexible bladed knife. Cool completely.

Chop the chocolate into small, evenly sized pieces and place in a heatproof bowl. Bring a saucepan of water to a boil, then remove from the heat. Sit the bowl over the saucepan, ensuring the bowl doesn't touch the water. Stand, stirring occasionally, until the chocolate has melted. Cool slightly.

Beat the cream until thick. Gently fold in the chocolate until well combined—do not overmix or it will curdle. Spread evenly over the base and refrigerate for 3 hours or until set. Remove from the pan and dust with the cocoa.

Makes 24 pieces

Gingerbread apricot upside-down cake

¾ cup glacé apricots
¾ cup unsalted butter
⅓ cup pecans, finely chopped
¾ cup firmly packed light brown
  sugar
¼ cup golden syrup or dark corn
  syrup
1½ cups self-rising flour
3 teaspoons ground ginger
½ teaspoon ground nutmeg

Preheat the oven to 350°F. Grease and flour the base of a deep, 8 inch round cake pan, shaking out the excess flour.

Arrange the apricots around the bottom of the pan, cut-side up. Melt the butter in a small saucepan over low heat. Transfer 1 tablespoon of the melted butter to a small bowl. Add the pecans and ¼ cup of the brown sugar and mix well. Sprinkle the mixture over the apricots.

Add the golden syrup and ½ cup water to the saucepan of melted butter and stir over medium heat until well combined. Sift the flour and spices in a bowl, then stir in the remaining sugar. Pour in the golden syrup mixture and mix well. Spoon the mixture over the apricots and smooth the surface.

Bake for 35–40 minutes or until a skewer comes out clean when inserted into the center of the cake. Leave in the pan for 15 minutes before unmolding and setting on a wire rack to cool. If desired, serve with custard.

Serves 6

Storage: This cake keeps for 4 days in an airtight container.

Walnut brownies

²/₃ cup self-rising flour
²/₃ cup cocoa powder
1 cup superfine sugar
1¹/₃ cups unsalted butter, melted
4 eggs, lightly beaten
1 teaspoon vanilla extract
1¹/₂ cups semisweet chocolate chips
1 cup walnut pieces
confectioners' sugar, to dust

Preheat the oven to 350°F. Grease a shallow, 12 x 8 inch baking pan and line with waxed paper, allowing the paper to hang over the two long sides of the pan.

Sift together the flour and cocoa, then add the sugar. Make a well in the center, then add the butter, eggs, and vanilla and beat until smooth. Fold in the chocolate chips and walnuts.

Spoon into the pan and smooth the surface. Bake for 25 minutes or until a skewer comes out clean. Leave in the pan for 10 minutes, then unmold and set on a wire rack to cool. Dust with confectioners' sugar.

Makes 24 pieces

Devil's food cake

1 1/3 cups all-purpose flour
2/3 cup cocoa powder
1 teaspoon baking soda
1 cup sugar
1 cup buttermilk
2 eggs, lightly beaten
1/2 cup unsalted butter, softened
1/2 cup heavy cream
confectioners' sugar, to dust
fresh berries, to garnish

Preheat the oven to 350°F. Grease a deep, 8 inch round cake pan and line the bottom with waxed paper. Sift the flour, cocoa, and baking soda into a large bowl.

Add the sugar to the sifted dry ingredients. Combine the buttermilk, eggs, and butter, then pour onto the dry ingredients. Beat with an electric mixer on low speed for 3 minutes or until just combined. Increase the speed to high and beat for 3 minutes or until the mixture is free of lumps and increased in volume. Spoon the mixture into the prepared pan and smooth the surface.

Bake for 40–50 minutes or until a skewer comes out clean when inserted into the center of the cake. Leave in the pan for 15 minutes before unmolding and setting on a wire rack to cool completely. Cut the cake in half horizontally and fill with whipped cream. Dust with confectioners' sugar and garnish with fresh berries.

Serves 8

Storage: Unfilled, the cake will keep for 3 days in an airtight container or up to 3 months in the freezer. The filled cake is best assembled and eaten on the day of baking.

Apple shortcake

2 cups all-purpose flour
1 teaspoon baking powder
½ cup unsalted butter, chilled
  and chopped
¼ cup superfine sugar
1 egg, lightly beaten
1 tablespoon cold milk
4 small red apples, peeled, quartered,
  and cored
1 teaspoon ground cinnamon
2 tablespoons superfine sugar, extra
1 tablespoon milk, extra
raw sugar, to sprinkle

Preheat the oven to 350°F. Lightly grease a cookie sheet and line with waxed paper, allowing paper to hang over the two long sides.

Sift the flour and baking powder into a large bowl, add the butter, and cut in with pastry blender or rub with your fingers until the mixture resembles fine bread crumbs. Stir in the sugar.

Make a well in the center and add the combined egg and milk. Mix with a flat-bladed knife using a cutting action until the mixture comes together in beads. Gently gather together and lift out onto a lightly floured work surface. Press together into a ball, flatten slightly, cover in plastic wrap, and chill for 20–30 minutes.

Halve the dough—keep one half in the refrigerator and roll the other half into an 8 inch square. Put on the cookie sheet. Cut the apple quarters into thin slices and arrange in rows to form a double layer of apples over the pastry. Sprinkle with the cinnamon and extra superfine sugar.

Roll the remaining pastry into an 8 inch square and put over the apples. Brush with milk and sprinkle with raw sugar. Bake for 40–45 minutes or until crisp and golden.

Makes 9 pieces

Panforte

³/₄ cup hazelnuts
³/₄ cup almonds
²/₃ cup candied citrus peel, chopped
²/₃ cup candied pineapple, chopped
grated zest of 1 lemon
²/₃ cup all-purpose flour
1 teaspoon ground cinnamon
¼ teaspoon ground coriander
¼ teaspoon ground cloves
¼ teaspoon grated nutmeg
pinch of white pepper
²/₃ cup sugar
4 tablespoons honey
¼ cup unsalted butter
confectioners' sugar, to dust

Line an 8 inch springform pan with rice paper or waxed paper and grease well with butter.

Toast the nuts under a broiler, turning them so they brown on all sides, then allow to cool. Put the nuts in a bowl with the candied peel, pineapple, lemon zest, flour, and spices and toss together. Preheat the oven to 300°F.

Put the sugar, honey, and butter in a saucepan and melt them together. Cook the syrup until it reaches 245°F on a sugar thermometer or a little of it dropped into cold water forms a firm ball when molded between your fingers (see page 393).

Pour the syrup into the nut mixture and mix well, working fast before it stiffens too much. Pour straight into the prepared pan, smooth the surface, and bake for 35 minutes. (Unlike other cakes, this cake will neither firm up as it cooks nor color at all, so you need to time it carefully.)

Cool in the pan until the cake firms up enough to remove the side of the pan. Peel off the paper and leave to cool completely. Dust the top with confectioners' sugar.

Serves 10

Squash fruitcake

1²/₃ cups squash, peeled and cut into
  small pieces
¹/₂ cup unsalted butter, softened
³/₄ cup light brown sugar
2 tablespoons golden syrup or dark
  corn syrup
2 eggs, lightly beaten
2 cups self-rising flour, sifted
1 cup mixed dried fruit
2 tablespoons chopped glacé ginger

Preheat the oven to 300°F. Grease a deep, 8 inch round cake pan and line the bottom and side with waxed paper.

Steam the squash for 10 minutes or until cooked through. Mash with a potato masher or a fork until smooth. Measure ³/₄ cup and set aside until ready to use.

Beat the butter and sugar together with an electric mixer until pale and creamy. Add the golden syrup and beat well. Gradually add the egg, beating well after each addition. Fold in the squash until combined. Combine the flour, dried fruit, and ginger, then fold into the butter mixture with a metal spoon until combined. Spoon the mixture into the prepared pan and smooth the surface.

Bake for 1 hour 40 minutes or until a skewer comes out clean when inserted into the center of the cake. Cool in the pan for 20 minutes before unmolding and setting on a wire rack.

Serves 8–10

Snickerdoodle bars

2 cups all-purpose flour
1 cup superfine sugar
1 tablespoon ground cinnamon
2 teaspoons baking powder
2 eggs
1 cup milk
1/2 cup unsalted butter, melted
3 tablespoons sugar
3 teaspoons ground cinnamon, extra

Preheat the oven to 350°F. Lightly grease a 12 x 8 inch baking pan and line with waxed paper, allowing paper to hang over the two long sides.

Sift together the flour, superfine sugar, cinnamon, and baking powder and make a well in the center. In a small bowl, whisk together the eggs and milk. Pour into the flour and mix with a metal spoon to roughly combine. Fold in the butter until smooth—do not overmix. Spoon half the mixture into the pan and level the surface.

Combine the sugar and extra cinnamon and sprinkle two thirds over the mixture in the pan. Gently spoon the remaining mixture over the top, then sprinkle the remaining cinnamon sugar over the surface. Bake for 25–30 minutes or until firm. Cool in the pan for 20 minutes, then transfer to a wire rack to cool.

Makes 20 pieces

Carrot, spice, and sour cream cake

2½ cups self-rising flour
2 teaspoons ground cinnamon
1 teaspoon ground nutmeg
¾ cup dark brown sugar
1⅓ cups grated carrot
4 eggs
1 cup sour cream
1 cup vegetable oil

Orange cream-cheese frosting
¼ cup cream cheese, softened
1 tablespoon unsalted butter,
  softened
1 teaspoon grated orange zest
2 teaspoons orange juice
1 cup confectioners' sugar

Preheat the oven to 315°F. Grease a deep, 8½ inch round pan and line the bottom with waxed paper. Sift the flour and spices into a large bowl, then stir in the brown sugar and grated carrot until well mixed.

Combine the eggs, sour cream, and oil until lightly beaten. Add to the carrot mixture and stir until well combined. Spoon the mixture into the prepared pan and smooth the surface.

Bake for 1 hour 15 minutes or until a skewer comes out clean when inserted into the center of the cake. Leave in the pan for 10 minutes before unmolding and setting on a wire rack to cool.

To make the frosting, beat the cream cheese, butter, zest, and juice in a bowl with an electric mixer until light and fluffy. Gradually beat in the confectioners' sugar until smooth. Spread over the cooled cake.

Serves 8–10

Mini mango cakes with lime syrup

15 oz. can mango slices in syrup, drained
1/3 cup unsalted butter, softened
3/4 cup superfine sugar
2 eggs, lightly beaten
1/2 cup self-rising flour
2 tablespoons ground almonds
2 tablespoons coconut milk
2 tablespoons lime juice

Preheat the oven to 400°F. Grease four jumbo muffin cups and line with mango slices. Beat the butter and 1/2 cup of the sugar in a bowl with an electric mixer until light and creamy. Gradually add the beaten eggs, beating well after each addition. Fold in the sifted flour, add the almonds and coconut milk, then spoon into the muffin cups. Bake for 25 minutes or until a skewer comes out clean when inserted into the center of the cakes.

To make the syrup, place the lime juice, the remaining sugar, and 1/2 cup water in a small saucepan and stir over low heat until the sugar dissolves. Increase the heat and simmer for 10 minutes. Pierce holes in each cake with a skewer. Drizzle the syrup over the top and allow to rest for 5 minutes to soak up the liquid. Turn out and serve.

Makes 4

Apple and berry crumble muffins

1 1/4 cups self-rising flour
1 cup whole-wheat flour
1 teaspoon baking powder
1/4 teaspoon ground cinnamon
pinch ground cloves
1/2 cup firmly packed light brown
   sugar
3/4 cup milk
2 eggs
1/2 cup unsalted butter, melted
   and cooled
2 Granny Smith apples, peeled,
   cored, and grated
1 cup blueberries

Crumble
5 tablespoons all-purpose flour
1/4 cup raw sugar
1/3 cup rolled oats
2 1/2 tablespoons unsalted butter,
   chopped

Preheat the oven to 375°F. Line twelve standard muffin cups with paper liners. Sift the flours, baking powder, cinnamon, and cloves into a large bowl and stir in the sugar. Make a well in the center.

Put the milk, eggs, and butter in a bowl, whisk, and pour into the well. Fold gently until just combined—the batter should be lumpy. Fold in the fruit. Divide among the muffin cups.

To make the crumble, put the flour, sugar, and oats in a bowl. Add the butter, cutting in with pastry blender or rubbing in with your fingertips until most of the lumps are gone. Sprinkle 2 teaspoons of the crumble over each muffin. Bake for 25 minutes or until golden. Cool for 5 minutes, then transfer to a wire rack.

Makes 12 regular muffins

Apricot and raisin bran loaf

3/4 cup dried apricots, chopped
1 cup raisins
1 cup bran cereal
1/2 cup light brown sugar
1 1/2 cups warm milk
1 cup self-rising flour, sifted
1/2 cup whole-wheat flour, sifted
1/2 teaspoon baking powder
1 teaspoon pumpkin pie spice

Preheat the oven to 350°F. Grease a deep, 7 x 4 inch loaf pan and line the bottom and sides with waxed paper.

Soak the apricots, raisins, bran cereal, and brown sugar in the milk in a large bowl for 30 minutes or until the milk is almost completely absorbed. Stir in the flours and pumpkin pie spice to form a stiff, moist batter. Spoon the mixture into the pan and smooth the surface.

Bake for 50 minutes or until a skewer comes out clean when inserted into the center of the cake—cover with aluminum foil during cooking if it browns too much. Leave in the pan for 10 minutes, then unmold and set on a wire rack to cool. Cut into thick slices. If desired, serve with butter and dust with confectioners' sugar.

Serves 6–8

Note: Use any dried fruit combination. This loaf is delicious toasted.

Berry and apple bars

²/₃ cup unsalted butter
1 ¹/₃ cups superfine sugar
2 eggs, lightly beaten
2 cups self-rising flour, sifted
²/₃ cup buttermilk
1 teaspoon vanilla extract
2 large apples
1 cup blueberries
1 ¹/₄ cups blackberries
confectioners' sugar, to dust

Preheat the oven to 350°F. Lightly grease a shallow, 12 x 8 inch baking pan and line with waxed paper, allowing paper to hang over the two long sides.

Beat the butter and sugar with an electric mixer until light and fluffy. Add the egg gradually, beating well after each addition. Stir in the flour and buttermilk alternately and mix until smooth. Stir in the vanilla. Spread an inch of mixture over the bottom of the pan.

Peel, quarter, and core the apples. Cut into very thin slices and arrange on the mixture. Spoon the remaining mixture over the apples and smooth the surface, then sprinkle with the blueberries and blackberries. Bake on the middle rack for 40 minutes or until cooked and golden.

Cool in the pan for 30 minutes before transferring to a wire rack. When completely cooled, dust with confectioners' sugar and cut into squares.

Makes 12 pieces

Walnut cake with chocolate icing

3/4 cup unsalted butter, softened
1/2 cup light brown sugar
2 eggs
1 1/2 cups self-rising flour
3/4 cup chopped walnuts
1/4 cup milk

Chocolate icing
4 oz. good-quality semisweet
   chocolate, chopped
1 tablespoon unsalted butter

Preheat the oven to 350°F. Grease an 8 inch springform pan and line the bottom with waxed paper.

Place the butter and sugar in a large bowl. Beat with an electric mixer for 5 minutes or until thick and creamy. Add the eggs one at a time, beating well after each addition. Fold in the flour and 1/2 cup of the walnuts alternately with the milk until just combined. Spoon the mixture into the prepared pan and smooth the surface.

Bake for 35 minutes or until a skewer comes out clean when inserted into the center of the cake. Leave in the pan for 5 minutes before unmolding and setting on a wire rack to cool.

To make the chocolate icing, put the chocolate and butter in a heatproof bowl. Bring a saucepan of water to a boil, then reduce the heat to a gentle simmer. Position the bowl over the saucepan, making sure the bottom of the bowl does not touch the water. Stir occasionally to ensure even melting. Cool slightly, then spread over the cake. Sprinkle with the remaining walnuts.

Serves 6

Florentines

¼ cup unsalted butter
¼ cup light brown sugar
2 teaspoons honey
¼ cup sliced almonds, roughly
  chopped
2 tablespoons chopped dried apricots
2 tablespoons chopped glacé
  cherries
2 tablespoons candied citrus peel
⅓ cup all-purpose flour, sifted
4 oz. semisweet chocolate

Preheat the oven to 350°F. Melt the butter, brown sugar, and honey in a saucepan until the butter is melted and all the ingredients are combined. Remove from the heat and add the almonds, apricots, glacé cherries, candied citrus peel, and the flour. Mix well.

Grease and line two cookie sheets with waxed paper. Place level tablespoons of the mixture well apart on the cookie sheets. Reshape and flatten the cookies into 2 inch rounds before cooking.

Bake for 10 minutes or until lightly browned. Cool on the cookie sheets, then allow to cool completely on a wire rack.

To melt the chocolate, break it up into small pieces and put it in a heatproof bowl. Bring a saucepan of water to a simmer, remove from the heat, and place the bowl over the saucepan. Stir the chocolate until melted. Spread the melted chocolate on the bottom of each Florentine and, using a fork, make a wavy pattern on the chocolate before it sets. Let the chocolate set before serving.

Makes 12

Lemon semolina cake

6 eggs, separated
1¼ cups superfine sugar
2 teaspoons finely grated lemon zest
⅓ cup lemon juice
¾ cup semolina
1 cup ground almonds
2 tablespoons self-rising flour
heavy cream, to serve

Preheat the oven to 325°F. Grease a 9½ inch springform pan and line the bottom with waxed paper. Place the egg yolks, 1 cup of the sugar, the lemon zest, and 2 tablespoons of the lemon juice in a large bowl. Beat with an electric mixer for 8 minutes or until thick and pale and the mixture leaves a trail when the mixer is lifted.

Beat the egg whites in a clean bowl with a clean electric mixer until firm peaks form. Gently fold the whites into the egg yolk mixture alternately with the combined semolina, ground almonds, and flour—do not overmix or the mixture will deflate. Carefully pour into the pan and smooth the surface. Bake for 35–40 minutes or until a skewer comes out clean when inserted into the center of the cake. Leave for 5 minutes in the pan, then unmold and set on a wire rack. Pierce a few holes in the cake with a skewer.

Place the remaining lemon juice and sugar in a small saucepan with ½ cup water. Stir over low heat until the sugar has dissolved. Increase the heat and simmer for 3 minutes or until thick and syrupy. Pour the hot syrup over the cooled cake. Serve with whipped cream.

Serves 8–10

Sesame and ginger bars

1 cup all-purpose flour
1/2 teaspoon baking soda
1 teaspoon ground ginger
1/4 teaspoon pumpkin pie spice
2 eggs
3/4 cup light brown sugar
1/2 cup unsalted butter, melted
1/4 cup chopped crystallized ginger
1/3 cup sesame seeds, toasted

Preheat the oven to 350°F. Lightly grease a shallow, 12 x 8 inch baking pan and line with waxed paper, allowing the paper to hang over the two long sides.

Sift together the flour, baking soda, ginger, pumpkin pie spice, and 1/4 teaspoon salt. Beat the eggs and brown sugar in a large bowl for 2 minutes or until thick and creamy. Mix in the melted butter and gently fold in the flour mixture. Add the crystallized ginger and half the sesame seeds and mix gently.

Spread into the pan and sprinkle evenly with the remaining sesame seeds. Bake for 20 minutes or until firm to the touch and slightly colored. Cool in the pan for 10 minutes, then cool on a wire rack.

Makes 15 pieces

Chocolate, almond, and candied citrus peel cake

1 tablespoon candied citrus peel, chopped
5 oz. semisweet chocolate pieces
1 cup ground almonds
1/2 cup self-rising flour
4 eggs, separated
1/2 cup superfine sugar
2 tablespoons warm milk
2/3 cup heavy cream

Preheat the oven to 350°F. Grease an 8 inch springform pan and line the base with waxed paper. Combine the candied citrus peel and 3 1/2 oz. of the chocolate in a food processor until finely ground. Add the ground almonds and flour and process briefly to combine.

Beat the egg yolks and sugar with an electric mixer for 5 minutes or until thick and pale—the mixers should leave a trail in the mixture. Stir in the chocolate and peel mixture, then the milk. Beat the egg whites in a clean bowl until soft peaks form. Gently fold the whites into the cake mixture with a metal spoon—do not overmix or it will lose volume. Pour the mixture into the pan and smooth the surface. Bake for 45 minutes or until a skewer comes out clean when inserted into the center of the cake. Leave in the pan for 5 minutes, then unmold and set on a wire rack to cool.

To make the filling, melt the remaining chocolate pieces in a heatproof bowl over a saucepan of hot water. Cut the cake in half horizontally. Spread the bottom layer with melted chocolate, then the whipped cream. Cover with the remaining layer and, if desired, dust with confectioners' sugar in a pattern.

Serves 6

Sticky gingerbread muffins

2 cups self-rising flour, sifted
$3/4$ cup all-purpose flour, sifted
$1/2$ teaspoon baking soda
3 teaspoons ground ginger
1 teaspoon ground cinnamon
1 teaspoon pumpkin pie spice
1 cup firmly packed light brown sugar
$1/4$ cup chopped glacé ginger
$2/3$ cup golden syrup or dark corn
   syrup
$1/3$ cup unsalted butter, chopped
1 cup buttermilk
1 egg, lightly beaten
2 oz. semisweet chocolate, chopped
   into evenly sized pieces, melted
   (see page 390)

Ginger frosting
$1/4$ cup unsalted butter, softened
$1 1/2$ tablespoons golden syrup or dark
   corn syrup
1 cup confectioners' sugar
$1/2$ teaspoon ground ginger

Preheat the oven to 400°F. Grease twelve standard muffin cups. Put the flours, baking soda, ginger, cinnamon, and pumpkin pie spice into a large bowl and stir in the brown sugar and glacé ginger. Make a well in the center. Melt the golden syrup and butter in a saucepan, stirring until well mixed. Cool. Combine the golden syrup mixture, buttermilk, and egg in a large bowl, mix together, and pour into the well. Fold until just combined—the batter will be lumpy.

Divide the mixture among the muffin cups. Bake for 20–25 minutes or until the muffins come away from the side of the pan. Cool for 5 minutes in the pan, then transfer to a wire rack.

To make the ginger frosting, beat the butter, golden syrup, confectioners' sugar, and ground ginger together with an electric mixer in a bowl until light and fluffy. Spread over the top of the muffins.

Spoon the melted chocolate into the corner of a plastic bag. Snip off the corner to create an opening for piping. Pipe the chocolate over the icing in crisscrossing lines. Apply even pressure and move at a steady speed to keep the chocolate from coagulating. Allow the chocolate to set before serving.

Makes 12 muffins

Bakewell bars

1 cup all-purpose flour
¼ cup confectioners' sugar
⅔ cup unsalted butter, chilled
  and chopped
1 egg yolk
½ cup superfine sugar
4 eggs
1¼ cups ground almonds
2 drops almond extract
½ cup raspberry preserves
¼ cup flaked almonds

Preheat the oven to 350°F. Lightly grease a 12 x 8 inch baking pan and line with waxed paper, allowing paper to hang over the two long sides.

Sift the flour and 1 tablespoon of the confectioners' sugar into a bowl, add ¼ cup of the butter, and cut it in with a pastry blender or rub in with your fingertips until the mixture resembles bread crumbs. Add the egg yolk and 2 tablespoons cold water and mix with a flat-bladed knife until the mixture comes together in beads. Gather into a ball, cover with plastic wrap, and refrigerate for 30 minutes. Roll out between two sheets of waxed paper, remove the paper, and put in the pan, pressing into the edges. Bake for 10 minutes. Allow to cool.

Beat the remaining butter and the superfine sugar with an electric mixer until creamy. Add the eggs and fold in the ground almonds and almond extract. Spread the preserves over the pastry base and pour the filling on top. Sprinkle with almonds and bake for 30–35 minutes or until firm. Cool.

Sift the remaining confectioners' sugar into a bowl and mix in 2–3 teaspoons warm water to form a free-flowing paste. Drizzle over the top in a zigzag pattern and allow to set. Trim the edges and cut into squares.

Makes 15 pieces

Orange poppy seed cake with citrus icing

⅓ cup poppy seeds
¾ cup warm milk
1 cup superfine sugar
3 eggs
2 cups self-rising flour, sifted
¾ cup plus 1 tablespoon unsalted butter, softened
1½ tablespoons finely grated orange zest
2 cups confectioners' sugar
heavy cream, to serve

Preheat the oven to 350°F. Lightly grease a 9 inch fluted Bundt pan. Combine the poppy seeds and milk in a bowl and set aside for at least 15 minutes.

Place the superfine sugar, eggs, flour, ¾ cup of the butter, and 3 teaspoons of the orange zest in a large bowl. Add the poppy seed mixture and beat with an electric mixer on low speed until combined. Increase to medium speed and beat for 3 minutes or until the mixture is thick and pale. Pour the mixture evenly into the prepared pan.

Bake for 50 minutes or until a skewer comes out clean when inserted into the center of the cake. Leave in the pan for 5 minutes, then unmold and set on a wire rack.

To make the icing, melt the remaining butter, then place in a bowl with the confectioners' sugar, the remaining orange zest, and 3 tablespoons boiling water. Mix to make a soft icing, then spread over the warm cake and serve with thick cream.

Serves 8

Passion fruit and coconut cheese bars

3/4 cup slivered almonds
1 cup all-purpose flour
1 teaspoon baking powder
1/3 cup unsalted butter, chopped
1/2 cup superfine sugar
1 egg yolk
1/4 cup dried shredded coconut
3 cups cream cheese, softened
2 eggs
3/4 cup coconut milk
3 teaspoons vanilla extract
1/2 teaspoon lemon juice
3/4 cup superfine sugar, extra
3/4 cup sliced almonds, toasted
  (see page 390)

Topping
3/4 cup confectioners' sugar
2 1/2 tablespoons unsalted butter,
  softened
1 tablespoon cornstarch
2 tablespoons strained passion
  fruit juice

Finely chop the almonds in a food processor. Sift the flour and baking powder into a bowl. Cut the butter into the flour with a pastry blender until the mixture resembles bread crumbs. Stir in the almonds and sugar. Make a well in the center and add the egg yolk. Mix with a flat-bladed knife until the mixture comes together in beads. Remove to a lightly floured work surface and shape into a ball. Flatten slightly, cover in plastic wrap, and refrigerate for 30 minutes.

Preheat the oven to 325°F. Grease a 12 x 8 inch pan and line with waxed paper, allowing paper to hang over the two long sides. Roll the dough out to fit the pan and press in evenly. Sprinkle with the coconut and lightly press it in. Bake for 10 minutes and cool for 10 minutes. Combine the cream cheese and eggs in the food processor. Add coconut milk, vanilla, lemon juice, and the extra sugar and blend until smooth. Pour over the base. Bake for 40 minutes. Cool in the pan.

To make the topping, mix the confectioners' sugar and butter with a wooden spoon until smooth. Stir in the cornstarch, then the passion fruit juice. Mix until smooth, then spread over the top. Sprinkle with the toasted almonds. Allow to set, then cut into 2 inch squares.

Makes 24 pieces

Pecan and coffee biscotti

1 3/4 cups all-purpose flour
1/2 teaspoon baking powder
2/3 cup superfine sugar
1/4 cup unsalted butter
2 eggs
1/2 teaspoon vanilla extract
2 tablespoons instant coffee granules
1 1/3 cups pecans
1/2 teaspoon superfine sugar, extra

Preheat the oven to 350°F and line two cookie sheets with waxed paper. Put the sifted flour, baking powder, sugar, and a pinch of salt in a food processor and mix for 1–2 seconds. Add the butter and mix until the mixture resembles fine bread crumbs. Add the eggs and vanilla and process until smooth.

Transfer the dough to a well-floured surface and knead in the coffee and pecans. Divide into two equal portions and, using lightly floured hands, shape each into a log about 8 inches long. Place the logs on the cookie sheets and sprinkle with the extra sugar. Press the top of each log down gently to make an oval.

Bake for 35 minutes or until golden. Remove and set aside to cool for about 20 minutes. Reduce the oven temperature to 325°F.

Cut the logs into 1/2 inch slices. Turn the waxed paper over, then spread the biscotti well apart on the cookie sheet so that they do not touch. Return to the oven and bake for 30 minutes or until they just begin to turn golden. Cool completely before storing in an airtight container.

Makes 40

Caramel peach cake

1 cup unsalted butter, softened
⅓ cup light brown sugar
1 lb. 11 oz. can peach halves in
  natural juice
1 cup superfine sugar
3 teaspoons finely grated lemon zest
3 eggs, lightly beaten
2½ cups self-rising flour, sifted
1 cup plain yogurt

Preheat the oven to 350°F. Grease a deep, 9 inch round cake pan and line the bottom with waxed paper. Melt ¼ cup of the butter and pour on the bottom of the pan. Evenly sprinkle the brown sugar over the top. Drain the peaches, reserving 1 tablespoon of the liquid. Arrange the peach halves, cut-side up, over the sugar mixture.

Beat the superfine sugar, lemon zest, and remaining butter with an electric mixer for 5–6 minutes or until pale and creamy. Add the egg gradually, beating well after each addition—the mixture may look curdled, but once you add the flour, it will come back together. Using a metal spoon, fold in the flour alternately with the yogurt (in two batches), then the reserved peach liquid. Spoon the mixture over the peaches and smooth the surface.

Bake for 1 hour 25 minutes or until a skewer comes out clean when inserted into the center of the cake. Cool in the pan for 30 minutes before unmolding and setting on a large serving plate.

Serves 10–12

Orange, pistachio, and semolina bars

$^2/_3$ cup shelled pistachio nuts
$^3/_4$ cup unsalted butter, chopped
$^2/_3$ cup superfine sugar
1 teaspoon vanilla extract
1 tablespoon finely grated orange zest
2 eggs
$^1/_2$ cup self-rising flour, sifted
$^1/_2$ cup orange juice
$1^1/_2$ cups fine semolina
1 cup superfine sugar, extra
$^1/_2$ cup orange juice, extra
confectioners' sugar, to dust

Preheat the oven to 350°F. Lightly grease a shallow, 12 x 8 inch baking pan and line with waxed paper, allowing the paper to hang over on the two long sides.

Bake the pistachios for 8–10 minutes or until they are lightly toasted. Cool, then chop.

Beat the butter and sugar with an electric mixer until light and fluffy. Add the vanilla, orange zest, and eggs and beat until combined.

Add the flour, orange juice, semolina, and pistachios and fold in with a spatula until just combined—do not overmix. Spread into the pan. Bake for 30 minutes or until golden brown and firm when lightly touched. Cool for 10 minutes in the pan, then on a wire rack placed on a cookie sheet.

Mix the extra sugar and orange juice in a small saucepan. Bring to a boil over medium heat, then simmer for 1 minute. Spoon over the top. Cool and cut into squares or diamonds. Dust with confectioners' sugar.

Makes 18 pieces

Raisin butter cake

1 cup raisins
1/4 cup rum
1 tablespoon light brown sugar
1 cup unsalted butter, softened
1 cup firmly packed light brown
  sugar, extra
3 eggs, lightly beaten
2 1/2 cups self-rising flour, sifted
3/4 cup buttermilk

Coffee butter frosting
3 teaspoons instant coffee powder
1/2 cup unsalted butter, softened
1 1/2 cups confectioners' sugar, sifted
1/2 teaspoon vanilla extract
2 teaspoons milk

Preheat the oven to 350°F. Lightly grease a 9 inch round cake pan and line the bottom with waxed paper. Combine the raisins, rum, and brown sugar in a small saucepan. Bring to a boil, reduce the heat, and simmer for 30 seconds or until the rum is absorbed. Set aside to cool.

Beat the butter and extra brown sugar with an electric mixer until pale and creamy. Add the egg gradually, beating well after each addition—the mixture may look curdled, but once you add the flour it will come back together. Using a metal spoon, fold in the flour and buttermilk in two batches, then fold in the raisin and rum mixture.

Spoon the mixture into the pan and bake for 1 hour 30 minutes or until a skewer comes out clean when inserted into the center of the cake. Leave in the pan for 10 minutes before unmolding and setting on a wire rack to cool.

To make the frosting, dissolve the coffee in 2 tablespoons boiling water. Beat the butter and confectioners' sugar with an electric mixer until pale and creamy. Add the vanilla, coffee mixture, and milk and beat for 2 minutes or until smooth and fluffy. Spread over the cool cake.

Serves 10

Passion fruit melting moments

1 cup unsalted butter
⅓ cup confectioners' sugar
1 teaspoon vanilla extract
1½ cups self-rising flour
½ cup plain custard powder

Passion fruit filling
¼ cup unsalted butter
½ cup confectioners' sugar
1½ tablespoons passion fruit pulp

Preheat the oven to 350°F. Line two cookie sheets with waxed paper. Beat the butter and sugar until light and creamy. Beat in the vanilla extract. Sift in the flour and custard powder and mix to a soft dough. Roll level tablespoons of the mixture into twenty-eight balls and place on cookie sheets. Flatten slightly with a floured fork.

Bake for 20 minutes or until lightly golden. Cool on a wire rack.

To make the filling, beat the butter and sugar until light and creamy, then beat in the passion fruit pulp. Use the filling to sandwich the cookies together. Allow to firm before serving.

Makes 14 filled cookies

Variation: You can vary the flavor of the filling. To make a coffee filling, for example, dissolve 2 teaspoons of instant coffee in 2 teaspoons water and add to the butter and sugar mixture. Beat until well combined.

Apricot pine nut cake

²/₃ cup pine nuts, roughly chopped
1 cup unsalted butter, softened
1 cup sugar
3 teaspoons finely grated orange zest
3 eggs, lightly beaten
2¹/₂ cups self-rising flour, sifted
³/₄ cup glacé apricots, finely chopped
1 cup orange juice

Preheat the oven to 350°F. Lightly grease a 10¹/₂ inch round cake pan and line the bottom with waxed paper. Spread the pine nuts on a baking sheet and bake for 5–10 minutes or until lightly golden. Allow to cool.

Beat the butter, sugar, and orange zest with an electric mixer until pale and creamy. Add the egg gradually, beating well after each addition—the mixture may look curdled, but once you add the flour it will come back together. Fold in the sifted flour, pine nuts, apricots, and orange juice in two batches with a metal spoon. Spoon the mixture into the prepared pan and smooth the surface.

Bake for 1 hour 20 minutes or until a skewer comes out clean when inserted into the center of the cake. Leave in the pan for 10 minutes before unmolding and setting on a wire rack to cool. If desired, dust with confectioners' sugar and serve with cream or yogurt.

Serves 10

Note: The chopped apricots may form lumps—flour your hands and rub through to separate.
Variation: For a little extra flavor, add 2 tablespoons brandy to the cake mixture with the flour, pine nuts, apricots, and orange juice.

Quick banana bread

1 cup cream cheese, softened
1 cup raw sugar
3 large ripe bananas, mashed (about
    1 cup)
2 eggs, lightly beaten
10 oz. packet scone mix
½ cup chopped pecans

Preheat the oven to 350°F. Grease a 9 x 5 inch loaf pan and line the bottom and two long sides with a long sheet of waxed paper.

Beat the cream cheese and sugar in a large bowl with an electric mixer until light and smooth. Add the banana and eggs and beat for 2 minutes or until well combined. Fold in the scone mix and pecans until well combined.

Spoon the mixture into the prepared pan and smooth the surface. Bake for 40 minutes. Cover with aluminum foil and bake for another 15 minutes or until a skewer comes out clean when inserted into the center of the cake. Leave in the pan for 10 minutes before unmolding and setting on a wire rack to cool. Cool completely before serving.

Serves 12

Note: This banana bread may be served with or without butter. It will keep well for up to 5 days stored in an airtight container.

Chewy fruit and seed bars

³/₄ cup unsalted butter
½ cup golden syrup or dark corn
  syrup
½ cup crunchy peanut butter
2 teaspoons vanilla extract
¼ cup all-purpose flour
⅓ cup ground almonds
½ teaspoon pumpkin pie spice
3 cups quick-cooking oats
2 teaspoons finely grated orange zest
1 cup light brown sugar
½ cup dried shredded coconut
⅓ cup sesame seeds, toasted
½ cup pumpkin seeds or shelled
  sunflower seeds
½ cup raisins, chopped
¼ cup candied citrus peel

Preheat the oven to 325°F. Lightly grease a shallow, 12 x 8 inch pan and line with waxed paper, allowing paper to hang over the two long sides.

Place the butter and golden syrup in a small saucepan over low heat, stirring occasionally until melted. Remove from the heat and stir in the peanut butter and vanilla until combined.

Mix together the remaining ingredients, stirring well. Make a well in the center and add the butter and syrup mixture. Mix with a large metal spoon until combined. Press evenly into the pan and bake for 25 minutes or until golden and firm. Cool in the pan, then cut into squares.

Makes 18 pieces

Rich dark chocolate cake

3/4 cup unsalted butter, chopped
1 1/2 cups semisweet chocolate chips
1 3/4 cups self-rising flour
1/3 cup cocoa powder
1 1/2 cups superfine sugar
3 eggs, lightly beaten

Chocolate topping
1 tablespoon unsalted butter,
  chopped
4 oz. semisweet chocolate, chopped

Preheat the oven to 315°F. Grease an 8 1/2 inch springform pan and line the bottom with waxed paper. Place the butter and chocolate chips in a small heatproof bowl and melt, stirring frequently, over a saucepan of simmering water. Make sure the bottom of the bowl doesn't touch the water.

Sift the flour and cocoa into a large bowl. Combine the melted butter and chocolate mixture, sugar, and egg, then add 1 cup water and mix well. Add to the flour and cocoa and stir until well combined.

Pour the mixture into the prepared pan and bake for 1 hour 30 minutes or until a skewer comes out clean when inserted into the center of the cake. Leave in the pan for 15 minutes before unmolding and setting on a wire rack to cool.

To make the chocolate topping, place the butter and chocolate pieces in a small heatproof bowl and melt, stirring frequently, over a saucepan of simmering water—make sure the bottom of the bowl doesn't touch the water. Spread the topping over the cooled cake in a swirl pattern.

Serves 10–12

Chocolate chip cookies

½ cup unsalted butter
1 cup light brown sugar
1 teaspoon vanilla extract
1 egg, lightly beaten
1 tablespoon milk
1¾ cups all-purpose flour
1 teaspoon baking powder
1½ cups semisweet chocolate chips

Preheat the oven to 350°F. Line a large cookie sheet with waxed paper.

Cream the butter and sugar in a large bowl using an electric mixer. Mix in the vanilla and gradually add the egg, beating well. Stir in the milk. Sift the flour and baking powder into a large bowl, then fold into the butter and egg mixture. Stir in the chocolate chips with a large spoon.

Drop level tablespoons of the cookie dough onto the cookie sheet, leaving about 1½ inches between each cookie, then lightly press with a floured fork. Bake for 15 minutes or until lightly golden. Allow to cool on a wire rack.

Makes 16

Passion fruit and lemon bars

½ cup unsalted butter, softened
½ cup confectioners' sugar, sifted
½ teaspoon vanilla extract
1½ cups all-purpose flour, sifted
1 teaspoon grated lemon zest
confectioners' sugar, to dust

Filling
¾ cup all-purpose flour
½ teaspoon baking powder
¾ cup dried shredded coconut
3 eggs
1 cup superfine sugar
5½ oz. can passion fruit pulp
2 tablespoons lemon juice
1 teaspoon grated lemon zest

Preheat the oven to 350°F. Lightly grease an 11 x 7 inch baking pan and line with waxed paper, allowing the paper to hang over the two long sides.

Cream the butter and confectioners' sugar with an electric mixer until pale and creamy, then add the vanilla. Fold in the flour and lemon zest with a large metal spoon. Press into the pan and bake for 15–20 minutes or until pale golden.

To make the filling, sift the flour and baking powder together and add the coconut. Lightly beat the eggs and sugar in a bowl, then add the passion fruit pulp, lemon juice, and zest. Add the dry ingredients and stir until combined. Pour over the base and bake for 20 minutes or until firm to the touch. Cool in the pan. Dust with confectioners' sugar and cut into pieces.

Makes 18 pieces

Rum and raisin cake

1 1/4 cups raisins
1/4 cup dark rum
1 1/2 cups self-rising flour
2/3 cup unsalted butter, chopped
3/4 cup light brown sugar
3 eggs, lightly beaten
ice cream, to serve

Preheat the oven to 350°F. Grease a deep, 8 inch round cake pan and line the bottom with waxed paper. Soak the raisins and rum in a small bowl for 10 minutes. Sift the flour into a large bowl and make a well in the center.

Melt the butter and sugar in a small saucepan over low heat, stirring until the sugar has dissolved. Remove from the heat. Combine with the rum and raisin mixture and add to the flour with the egg. Stir with a wooden spoon until combined—do not overbeat. Spoon the mixture into the prepared pan and smooth the surface.

Bake for 40 minutes or until a skewer comes out clean when inserted into the center of the cake. Delicious served with ice cream.

Serves 8

Glacé fruit bars

2 cups roughly chopped glacé fruit
2 tablespoons rum
1/3 cup unsalted butter, softened
1/3 cup superfine sugar
2 eggs
2 teaspoons vanilla extract
1 cup mixed toasted nuts, roughly
  chopped
1/4 cup all-purpose flour, sifted
1/4 cup self-rising flour, sifted
1/4 cup powdered milk
2/3 cup confectioners' sugar
1 teaspoon rum, extra

Preheat the oven to 375°F. Lightly grease an shallow, 11 x 7 inch baking pan and line with waxed paper, allowing paper to hang over the two long sides.

Combine the glacé fruit and rum in a bowl. Beat the butter and sugar with an electric mixer until light and fluffy. Add the eggs one at a time, beating well after each addition. Beat in the vanilla, then stir in the fruit mixture, nuts, flours, and powdered milk.

Spread evenly into the pan. Bake for 15 minutes, then reduce the temperature to 350°F and bake for 10 minutes or until golden brown. Cool in the pan until just warm.

Combine the confectioners' sugar, extra rum, and 1 teaspoon water until smooth and spreadable but not runny. If the icing is too thick, add a little more rum or water. Spread over the top and cool completely. Cut into three strips lengthwise, then cut each strip into eight pieces.

Makes 24 pieces

Chocolate hazelnut friands

1 1/2 cups hazelnuts
3/4 cup unsalted butter
6 egg whites
1 1/4 cups all-purpose flour
1/4 cup cocoa powder
2 cups confectioners' sugar
confectioners' sugar, extra, to dust

Preheat the oven to 400°F. Grease twelve 1/2 cup friand or muffin cups. Spread the hazelnuts out on a cookie sheet and bake for 8–10 minutes or until fragrant (be careful not to burn). Put in a clean dish towel and rub vigorously to loosen the skins. Discard the skins. Cool, then process in a food processor until finely ground.

Place the butter in a small saucepan and melt over medium heat, then cook for 3–4 minutes or until it turns a deep golden color. Strain any dark solids and set aside to cool (the color will become deeper after cooling).

Lightly whisk the egg whites in a bowl until frothy but not firm. Sift the flour, cocoa powder, and confectioners' sugar into a large bowl and stir in the ground hazelnuts. Make a well in the center, add the egg whites and butter, and mix until combined.

Spoon the mixture into the friand cups until three-quarters filled. Bake for 20–25 minutes or until a skewer inserted into the center comes out clean. Leave in the pan for a few minutes, then cool on a wire rack. Dust with confectioners' sugar and serve.

Makes 12

Apple coffee cake

²/₃ cup unsalted butter, chopped
1 cup superfine sugar
2 eggs, lightly beaten
1 teaspoon vanilla extract
1½ cups self-rising flour, sifted
³/₄ cup vanilla yogurt
1 Granny Smith apple, peeled, cored,
   and thinly sliced
1 teaspoon ground cinnamon

Preheat the oven to 350°F. Grease a deep, 8 inch round cake pan and line the bottom with waxed paper. Beat ½ cup of the butter and ³/₄ cup of the sugar with an electric mixer until light and creamy.

Gradually add the beaten egg, beating well after each addition until combined. Add the vanilla extract. Fold in the flour, then the yogurt, and stir until smooth. Spoon the mixture into the prepared pan and smooth the surface.

Arrange the apple slices evenly over the mixture in a circular pattern, starting in the center. Sprinkle with the cinnamon and the remaining sugar. Melt the remaining butter, then drizzle over the top.

Bake for 1 hour or until a skewer comes out clean when inserted into the center of the cake. Leave in the pan for 30 minutes before unmolding and setting on a wire rack to cool. If desired, combine a little extra cinnamon and sugar and sprinkle over the apples.

Serves 8

Cider crumble bars

¼ cup unsalted butter
1½ tablespoons golden syrup or dark corn syrup
⅔ cup alcoholic apple cider
2 cups self-rising flour
⅛ teaspoon ground ginger
¼ cup light brown sugar
⅓ cup pitted dates, chopped
1½ cups walnuts, chopped
1 egg
1 large Granny Smith apple
2½ tablespoons superfine sugar
½ cup all-purpose flour

Preheat the oven to 325°F. Lightly grease a 12 x 8 inch baking pan and line with waxed paper, allowing paper to hang over the two long sides.

Melt 1 tablespoon of the butter and all the golden syrup in a saucepan. Remove from the heat and stir in the cider. Sift the flour and ginger into a bowl. Stir in the brown sugar, dates, and half the nuts. Beat in the golden syrup mixture and egg until smooth. Spoon into the pan.

Peel, core, and thinly slice the apple, then cut into ½ inch pieces. Melt the remaining butter in a small saucepan, add the superfine sugar, flour, apple, and remaining nuts, and stir well. Spread over the cake mixture. Bake for 30 minutes or until golden and a skewer comes out clean when inserted into the center of the cake. Cool in the pan, remove, and cut into squares.

Makes 24 pieces

Pineapple upside-down cake

1 tablespoon unsalted butter, melted
2 tablespoons firmly packed light
  brown sugar
1 lb. can pineapple rings in juice
1/3 cup unsalted butter, extra,
  softened
1/2 cup superfine sugar
2 eggs, lightly beaten
1 teaspoon vanilla extract
1 cup self-rising flour

Preheat the oven to 350°F. Grease an 8 inch ring mold. Pour the melted butter into the bottom of the pan and tip to coat evenly. Sprinkle with the brown sugar. Drain the pineapple and reserve 1/3 cup of the juice. Cut the pineapple rings in half and arrange on the bottom.

Beat the extra butter and the superfine sugar with an electric mixer until light and creamy. Gradually add the beaten eggs, beating well after each addition. Add the vanilla extract and beat until combined. Using a metal spoon, fold in the flour alternately with the reserved juice.

Spoon the mixture evenly over the pineapple and smooth the surface. Bake for 35–40 minutes or until a skewer comes out clean when inserted into the center of the cake. Leave in the pan for 10 minutes before unmolding and setting on a wire rack to cool.

Serves 6–8

Orange-scented date crescents

1 cup pitted dates, chopped
3 teaspoons finely grated orange zest
2 teaspoons orange blossom water or
　orange juice
1/2 cup unsalted butter, cubed and
　softened
1/2 cup superfine sugar
1 egg
2 cups all-purpose flour, sifted
1 teaspoon baking powder
sugar, to sprinkle

Put the dates and 1 tablespoon water in a small saucepan. Stir over low heat for 2–3 minutes or until the dates are soft. Remove from the heat and stir in 1 teaspoon of the zest and 1 teaspoon of the orange blossom water. Cool.

Line two cookie sheets with waxed paper. Beat the butter, superfine sugar, the remaining orange zest, and orange blossom water until creamy. Add the egg and beat until well combined.

Mix in the combined flour and baking powder until a smooth dough forms. Cover with plastic wrap and refrigerate for 30 minutes. Put half the dough between two sheets of waxed paper and roll out to 1/4 inch thick. Refrigerate again if the dough is too soft. Preheat the oven to 350°F.

Cut out ten 2 1/2 inch circles from the dough with a fluted cutter. Put a small teaspoon of filling onto each circle and fold over to form a crescent, gently pressing the edges to seal. The pastry should be well filled with the mixture. Repeat with the remaining dough.

Lay the crescents on the trays, brush the tops with water, and sprinkle with the sugar. Bake for 10–15 minutes or until pale golden. Cool on a wire rack.

Makes about 25

Saffron spice cake

1 cup freshly squeezed orange juice
1 tablespoon finely grated orange zest
1/4 teaspoon saffron threads
3 eggs
1 1/4 cups confectioners' sugar
2 cups self-rising flour
3 2/3 cups ground almonds
1/2 cup unsalted butter, melted
confectioners' sugar, extra, to dust
heavy cream, to serve

Preheat the oven to 350°F. Lightly grease a 9 inch round cake pan and line the bottom with waxed paper. Combine the orange juice, zest, and saffron in a small saucepan and bring to a boil. Lower the heat and simmer for 1 minute. Allow to cool.

Beat the eggs and confectioners' sugar with an electric mixer until light and creamy. Fold in the sifted flour, almonds, orange juice mixture, and butter with a metal spoon until just combined and the mixture is just smooth. Spoon the mixture into the prepared pan.

Bake for 1 hour or until a skewer comes out clean when inserted into the center of the cake. Leave in the pan for 15 minutes before unmolding and setting on a wire rack to cool. Dust with a little confectioners' sugar and serve with whipped cream.

Serves 8

Lemon squares

½ cup unsalted butter
⅓ cup superfine sugar
1¼ cups all-purpose flour, sifted
confectioners' sugar, to dust

Topping
4 eggs, lightly beaten
1 cup superfine sugar
¼ cup lemon juice
1 teaspoon finely grated lemon zest
¼ cup all-purpose flour
½ teaspoon baking powder

Preheat the oven to 350°F. Lightly grease a 12 x 8 inch baking pan and line with waxed paper, allowing the paper to hang over the two long sides.

Cream the butter and sugar with an electric mixer until pale and fluffy. Fold in the flour with a metal spoon. Press into the pan and bake for 20 minutes or until golden and firm. Allow to cool.

Beat the eggs and sugar with an electric mixer for 2 minutes or until light and fluffy. Stir in the lemon juice and lemon zest. Sift together the flour and baking powder and gradually whisk into the egg mixture. Pour onto the base. Bake for 25 minutes or until just firm. Cool in the pan and dust with confectioners' sugar.

Makes 30 pieces

Almond, orange, and cardamom biscotti

2 eggs
2/3 cup firmly packed soft brown sugar
1 cup self-rising flour
3/4 cup all-purpose flour
1 1/4 cups almonds
1 tablespoon finely grated orange zest
1/4 teaspoon ground cardamom

Preheat the oven to 315°F. Line a baking tray with waxed paper.

Beat the eggs and sugar in a bowl with an electric mixer until pale and creamy. Sift the flours into the bowl, then add the almonds, orange zest, and cardamom and mix to form a soft dough.

Turn out the dough onto a lightly floured work surface. Divide the mixture into two portions, shaping it into two 8 x 2 inch loaves.

Bake for 35–40 minutes or until lightly golden. Transfer to a wire rack to cool. Cut the loaves into 1/2 inch diagonal slices with a large, serrated bread knife. The biscotti will be crumbly on the edges, so work slowly and, if possible, try to hold the sides as you cut.

Arrange the slices on cookie sheets in a single layer. Return to the oven for 10 minutes on each side. Don't worry if they don't seem fully dry, as they will become crisp on cooling. Allow the biscotti to cool before serving.

Makes 40

Storage: Biscotti can be stored in an airtight container for 2–3 weeks.

Golden ginger pear cake

½ cup golden syrup or dark corn
 syrup
2 cups self-rising flour
2½ teaspoons ground ginger
¾ cup firmly packed light brown
 sugar
2 pears, peeled, halved, and thinly
 sliced
3 eggs, lightly beaten
½ cup buttermilk
⅔ cup unsalted butter, chopped

Preheat the oven to 350°F. Grease a deep, 7 inch round cake pan and line the bottom with waxed paper. Pour half of the golden syrup over the bottom of the pan, spreading evenly with a metal spoon that has been run under hot water.

Sift the flour and ground ginger into a bowl. Add the sugar and pears, then the beaten eggs, buttermilk, and ½ cup of the butter, melted, and stir until just combined and smooth.

Spoon the mixture into the prepared pan and bake for 1 hour 30 minutes or until a skewer comes out clean when inserted into the center of the cake. Leave in the pan for 10 minutes, then carefully invert onto a serving plate.

Heat the remaining golden syrup and butter in a saucepan over low heat until the butter has melted. Spoon the sauce evenly over the cake and serve warm. If desired, serve with ice cream or whipped cream.

Serves 8

Chocolate and glacé cherry bars

1 cup all-purpose flour
1/3 cup cocoa powder
1/3 cup superfine sugar
1/2 cup unsalted butter, melted
1 teaspoon vanilla extract
2 cups glacé cherries, finely chopped
1/2 cup confectioners' sugar
1 1/2 cups dried shredded coconut
1/2 cup condensed milk
1/4 cup unsalted butter, melted
1/4 cup vegetable shortening, melted
5 oz. semisweet baking chocolate
1 tablespoon unsalted butter, extra

Preheat the oven to 350°F. Lightly grease a shallow, 11 x 7 inch baking pan and line with waxed paper, allowing the paper to hang over the two long sides.

Sift the flour, cocoa, and sugar into a bowl, add the butter and vanilla, and mix to form a dough. Gather together and turn onto a well-floured surface. Press together for 1 minute, then press into the bottom of the pan. Chill for 20 minutes. Cover with waxed paper and baking beads or uncooked rice and bake for 10–15 minutes. Remove the paper and beads and bake for 5 minutes. Cool.

Combine the cherries, confectioners' sugar, and coconut. Stir in the condensed milk, butter, and shortening, then spread over the base. Chill for 30 minutes.

Chop the chocolate and extra butter into small, evenly sized pieces and place in a heatproof bowl. Bring a saucepan of water to a boil and remove from the heat. Position the bowl over the saucepan, making sure the bowl doesn't touch the water. Allow to rest, stirring occasionally until melted. Pour over the cooled cherry mixture, then chill until set.

Makes 28 pieces

Honey, banana, and macadamia cake

1/2 cup unsalted butter, chopped
1 1/4 cups honey
2 1/2 cups self-rising flour
1 1/2 teaspoons pumpkin pie spice
3 or 4 large carrots, coarsely grated
1 large ripe banana, mashed
3/4 cup macadamia nuts, chopped
3 eggs, lightly beaten

Ricotta honey icing
1 1/2 cups smooth ricotta cheese
1/4 cup unsalted butter, softened
2 tablespoons honey

Preheat the oven to 350°F. Grease a 10 1/2 inch round cake pan and line the bottom with waxed paper. Melt the butter and honey in a saucepan, stirring until combined. Allow to cool.

Sift the flour and pumpkin pie spice into a large bowl. Add the carrots, banana, macadamias, egg, and honey mixture, stirring until the mixture is just combined and smooth.

Spoon the mixture into the prepared pan and bake for 1 hour 10 minutes or until a skewer comes out clean when inserted into the center of the cake. Leave in the pan for 15 minutes before carefully unmolding and setting on a wire rack to cool.

To make the ricotta honey icing, beat the ricotta, butter, and honey with an electric mixer for 2–3 minutes or until light and creamy. Spread the icing over the top of the cake.

Serves 8–10

Chocolate peanut squares

7 oz. semisweet chocolate
1/2 cup unsalted butter
1 cup firmly packed light brown sugar
1/4 cup crunchy peanut butter
2 eggs
1 cup all-purpose flour
1/4 cup self-rising flour
1/2 cup unsalted roasted peanuts,
  roughly chopped
3 1/2 oz. semisweet chocolate, extra,
  broken into pieces

Preheat the oven to 325°F. Lightly grease an 11 x 7 inch baking pan and line with waxed paper, allowing paper to hang over the two long sides.

Chop the chocolate into small, evenly sized pieces and place in a heatproof bowl. Bring a saucepan of water to a boil and remove from the heat. Sit the bowl over the saucepan, ensuring the bowl doesn't touch the water. Allow to rest, stirring occasionally until melted. Allow to cool.

Cream the butter, sugar, and peanut butter with an electric mixer until thick. Add the eggs one at a time, beating well after each addition. Stir in the chocolate, sifted flours, and peanuts.

Spread the mixture into the pan and gently press the pieces of semisweet chocolate evenly into the surface. Bake for 30 minutes or until a skewer inserted into the center comes out clean. Cool in the pan.

Makes 24 pieces

Rhubarb yogurt cake

1¼ cups finely sliced fresh rhubarb
2½ cups self-rising flour, sifted
1 cup superfine sugar
1 teaspoon vanilla extract
2 eggs, lightly beaten
½ cup plain yogurt
1 tablespoon rosewater
½ cup unsalted butter, melted

Preheat the oven to 350°F. Lightly grease a 9 inch round cake pan and line the bottom with waxed paper. Combine the rhubarb, flour, and sugar in a bowl.

Add the vanilla extract, egg, yogurt, rosewater, and melted butter, stirring until the mixture is just combined.

Spoon the mixture into the cake pan and bake for 1 hour or until a skewer comes out clean when inserted into the center of the cake. Leave in the pan for 15 minutes before turning out onto a wire rack. Serve with yogurt or cream, if desired.

Serves 8

Almond shortbreads

1 cup unsalted butter
2 cups all-purpose flour
1 teaspoon baking powder
3/4 cup confectioners' sugar, sifted
1 egg yolk
1 teaspoon vanilla extract
1 tablespoon ouzo
3/4 cup slivered almonds, ground to a
   medium-fine texture
4 tablespoons ground almonds
1/2 cup confectioners' sugar, extra,
   to dust

Melt the butter over low heat in a small, heavy-bottomed saucepan without stirring or shaking the saucepan. Carefully pour the clear butter into another container, leaving the white sediment in the pan to be discarded. Refrigerate for 1 hour. Preheat the oven to 325°F and line two cookie sheets with waxed paper.

In a bowl, sift the flour and baking powder together. Using an electric mixer, beat the chilled butter until light and fluffy. Gradually add the confectioners' sugar and combine well. Add the egg yolk, vanilla, and ouzo and beat until just combined. Fold in the flour, the ground slivered almonds, and the ground almonds.

Shape heaping tablespoons of mixture into crescents, place on the cookie sheets, and bake for 12 minutes or until pale golden. Remove from the oven and dust liberally with confectioners' sugar. Cool a little on the cookie sheets.

Line a cookie sheet with waxed paper and dust the paper with confectioners' sugar. Lift the warm cookies onto this and dust again with confectioners' sugar. When the cookies are cool, dust them once again with confectioners' sugar before storing them in an airtight container.

Makes 22

Sour cherry cake

1/2 cup unsalted butter, softened
3/4 cup superfine sugar
2 eggs, lightly beaten
1 cup ground almonds
1 cup self-rising flour
1/2 cup all-purpose flour
1/2 cup milk
1 lb. 8 oz. jar pitted morello cherries,
    well drained

Preheat the oven to 350°F. Grease and flour a 9 inch, fluted Bundt pan, shaking out the excess flour.

Beat the butter and sugar with an electric mixer until pale but not creamy. Add the beaten eggs gradually, beating well after each addition.

Stir in the ground almonds, then fold in the sifted flours alternately with the milk. Gently fold in the cherries. Spoon the mixture into the prepared pan and smooth the surface.

Bake for 50 minutes or until a skewer comes out clean when inserted into the center of the cake. Allow to cool in the pan for 10 minutes before unmolding and setting on a wire rack to cool. If desired, dust with confectioners' sugar before serving.

Serves 8–10

Note: This cake is best eaten on the day it is made.

Italian orange cookies

1½ cups all-purpose flour
1⅔ cups semolina or fine polenta
½ cup superfine sugar
⅓ cup unsalted butter, softened
2½ teaspoons grated orange zest
2 eggs

Put the flour, semolina, sugar, butter, orange zest, eggs, and a pinch of salt in a food processor and mix until smooth. Chill the mixture in the refrigerator for 15 minutes.

Preheat the oven to 375°F. Grease a cookie sheet and place a teaspoon of the mixture on the cookie sheet. Lightly moisten your fingers with a little water and press the mixture down to flatten it. Don't use too much water or it will affect the texture of the cookies. Leave space between the cookies, as the cookies will expand during cooking.

Bake for 15 minutes or until the edges of the cookies are dark golden. Remove from the oven, lift off the tray with a metal spatula, and cool on a wire rack. If you are baking the cookies in batches, make sure the cookie sheet is greased each time you use it.

Makes 45

Orange and lemon syrup cake

3 lemons
3 oranges
1 cup unsalted butter, chilled and chopped
2¾ cups superfine sugar
6 eggs, lightly beaten
1½ cups milk
3 cups self-rising flour, sifted

Preheat the oven to 315°F. Grease a 9½ inch springform pan and line the bottom and side with waxed paper. Finely grate the zest from the lemons and oranges to give 3 tablespoons of each, then squeeze the fruit to give ¾ cup juice from each. Heat the butter, 2 cups of the sugar, and 1 tablespoon each of the lemon and orange zest in a saucepan over low heat, stirring until melted. Pour into a bowl.

Add half the beaten eggs, ¾ cup of the milk, and 1½ cups of the flour to the bowl, beating with an electric mixer until just combined. Add the remaining beaten egg, milk, and flour and beat until smooth—do not overmix. Pour into the pan and bake for 1 hour 15 minutes or until a skewer comes out clean when inserted into the center of the cake— cover with aluminum foil if it browns too much during baking. Cool in the pan.

Combine the fruit juices, the remaining zests and sugar, and ½ cup water in a saucepan and stir over low heat until the sugar has dissolved. Increase the heat and bring to a boil for 10 minutes or until it thickens and reduces slightly. Pour the hot syrup over the cool cake. Cool in the pan for 10 minutes, then remove.

Serves 10–12

Rum and raisin bars

½ cup raisins
⅓ cup dark rum
7 oz. semisweet chocolate
¼ cup unsalted butter
½ cup superfine sugar
1 cup heavy cream
1 cup all-purpose flour
3 eggs, lightly beaten
cocoa powder, to dust

Preheat the oven to 350°F. Lightly grease a shallow, 11 x 7 inch baking pan and line with waxed paper, allowing paper to hang over the two long sides.

Combine the raisins and rum. Chop the chocolate and butter into small, evenly sized pieces and place in a heatproof bowl. Bring a saucepan of water to a boil and remove from the heat. Position the bowl over the saucepan, ensuring the bowl doesn't touch the water. Allow to rest, stirring occasionally until melted. Stir in the superfine sugar and cream.

Sift the flour into a bowl. Add the raisins, chocolate mixture, and eggs and mix well. Pour into the pan and smooth the surface. Bake for 25–30 minutes or until just set. Cool completely, then refrigerate overnight before cutting into small pieces. Sprinkle liberally with cocoa powder.

Makes 20 pieces

Blueberry muffins

3 cups all-purpose flour
1 tablespoon baking powder
3/4 cup firmly packed light brown
  sugar
1/2 cup unsalted butter, melted
2 eggs, lightly beaten
1 cup milk
1 1/4 cups fresh or thawed frozen
  blueberries

Preheat the oven to 415°F. Grease or brush twelve standard muffin cups with melted butter or oil. Sift the flour and baking powder into a large bowl. Stir in the sugar and make a well in the center.

Add the combined melted butter, eggs, and milk all at once and fold until just combined. Do not overmix—the batter should look quite lumpy.

Fold in the blueberries. Spoon the batter into the prepared pan. Bake for 20 minutes or until golden brown. Cool on a wire rack.

Makes 12

Pear upside-down cake

2 tablespoons light brown sugar
15 oz. can pear halves in syrup
2 cups self-rising flour
$1/2$ cup unsalted butter
$3/4$ cup superfine sugar
2 eggs, lightly beaten

Preheat the oven to 350°F. Grease a 9 x 5 inch loaf pan and line the bottom with waxed paper. Sprinkle the brown sugar evenly over the bottom of the pan. Drain the pears and reserve the syrup. Cut the pears in half and arrange, cut-side down, over the bottom.

Sift the flour into a large bowl and make a well in the center. Melt the butter and superfine sugar in a small saucepan over low heat, stirring until the sugar has dissolved. Remove from the heat. Combine the beaten eggs with the reserved syrup. Add both the butter and the egg mixtures to the flour and stir with a wooden spoon until combined—do not overbeat. Spoon the mixture over the pears and smooth the surface.

Bake for 50 minutes or until a skewer comes out clean when inserted into the center of the cake. Leave in the pan for 15 minutes (this resting time allows the pears to adhere better to the cake) before unmolding and setting on a wire rack to cool.

Serves 6–8

Peanut toffee shortbread

1 1/4 cups unsalted butter
1/2 cup superfine sugar
1 egg
1 1/2 cups all-purpose flour, sifted
1/2 cup self-rising flour, sifted
1 cup light brown sugar
2 tablespoons golden syrup or dark
   corn syrup
1/2 teaspoon lemon juice
2 1/2 cups roasted unsalted peanuts

Preheat the oven to 350°F. Lightly grease an 11 x 7 inch baking pan and line the bottom and sides with waxed paper, allowing the paper to hang over the two long sides.

Cream 1/3 cup of butter and the superfine sugar with an electric mixer until light and fluffy. Add the egg and beat well. Fold in the sifted flours with a large metal spoon until just combined. Press into the pan and bake for 15 minutes or until firm and pale golden. Cool for 10 minutes.

Place the brown sugar, golden syrup, lemon juice, and remaining butter in a saucepan. Stir over low heat until the sugar has dissolved. Simmer, stirring, for 5 minutes. Stir in the peanuts. Spread evenly over the base using two spoons—be careful, as the mixture is very hot. Bake for another 5 minutes. Allow to cool in the pan for 15 minutes, then unmold and cut into slices.

Makes 18 pieces

Blueberry shortcake

3/4 cup hazelnuts
2 1/4 cups self-rising flour
1 1/2 teaspoons ground cinnamon
3/4 cup raw sugar
2/3 cup unsalted butter, chopped
2 eggs
1/2 cup blueberry preserves
1 tablespoon raw sugar, extra

Preheat the oven to 350°F. Grease a deep, 8 inch round cake pan and line the bottom with waxed paper. Spread the hazelnuts on a cookie sheet and bake them for 5–10 minutes or until pale golden. Place in a clean dish towel and rub together to remove the skins, then roughly chop.

Mix the flour, cinnamon, sugar, butter, and half the hazelnuts in a food processor in short bursts until finely chopped. Add the eggs and process until well combined. Press half the mixture onto the bottom of the pan, then spread the preserves evenly over the mixture. Lightly knead the remaining hazelnuts into the remaining dough, then press evenly over the blueberry layer.

Sprinkle the extra sugar over the top and bake for 50 minutes or until a skewer comes out clean when inserted into the center of the cake. Leave in the pan for 15 minutes before carefully unmolding and setting on a wire rack to cool. If desired, garnish with fresh blueberries and serve with whipped cream.

Serves 8–10

Peppermint and chocolate bars

1³/₄ cups all-purpose flour
1 teaspoon baking powder
¹/₂ cup soft brown sugar
³/₄ cup unsalted butter, melted
¹/₄ cup white vegetable shortening
3¹/₂ cups confectioners' sugar, sifted
1 teaspoon peppermint extract
2 tablespoons milk
2 tablespoons whipping cream
10 oz. semisweet baking chocolate
¹/₄ cup unsalted butter, extra

Preheat the oven to 350°F. Grease a 12 x 8 inch baking pan and line with waxed paper, allowing the paper to hang over the two long sides of the pan.

Sift together the flour and baking powder and add the brown sugar. Stir in the melted butter, press into the pan, and bake for 20 minutes. Cool.

Melt the shortening in a saucepan over medium heat. Stir in the confectioners' sugar, peppermint extract, milk, and whipping cream. Mix well and pour over the pastry base. Allow to set.

Chop the chocolate and extra butter into small, evenly sized pieces and place in a heatproof bowl. Bring a saucepan of water to a boil and remove from the heat. Position the bowl over the saucepan, making sure the bowl doesn't touch the water. Rest, stirring occasionally, until melted and combined. Cool slightly, then spread the icing on top. Chill until set, then cut into pieces.

Makes 20 pieces

Chocolate and almond torte

1 2/3 cups sliced or 1 cup whole
  almonds
1 slice pandoro sweet cake or 1 small
  brioche (about 1 1/2 oz.)
10 oz. semisweet chocolate
2 tablespoons brandy
2/3 cup unsalted butter, softened
2/3 cup superfine sugar
4 eggs
1 teaspoon vanilla extract (optional)
1 cup mascarpone
cocoa powder, to dust
crème fraîche, to serve

Preheat the oven to 325°F. Toast the almonds in the oven for 8–10 minutes until golden brown, being careful not to burn them.

Put the almonds and pandoro in a food processor and process until the mixture resembles coarse bread crumbs. Grease a 9 inch springform pan with butter. Transfer some of the mixture to the pan and shake it around to coat the bottom and side. Put the remaining nut mixture aside.

Gently melt the chocolate and brandy in a heatproof bowl set over a saucepan of simmering water, making sure the bowl does not touch the water. Stir occasionally until the chocolate has melted—do not overstir or the cocoa butter in the chocolate can separate. Cool slightly.

Cream the butter and sugar in the food processor until light and pale. Add the chocolate, eggs, vanilla, and mascarpone. Add the remaining nut mixture and mix well. Transfer to the pan.

Bake for 50–60 minutes or until just set. Rest in the pan for 15 minutes before taking out. Dust with a little cocoa when cool and serve with crème fraîche.

Serves 8

Banana and honey loaf

½ cup unsalted butter, softened
¾ cup light brown sugar
2 eggs, lightly beaten
2 tablespoons honey
1 large ripe banana, cut into chunks
1½ cups whole-wheat flour
1½ teaspoons baking powder
2 teaspoons ground cinnamon

Preheat the oven to 350°F. Grease a 9 x 5 inch loaf pan. Combine the butter and sugar in a food processor for 1 minute or until lighter in color. Add the beaten eggs and process until combined.

Put 1 tablespoon of the honey in a saucepan over low heat and warm for 1 minute or until runny. Add to the food processor with the banana and blend until smooth. Add the flour and cinnamon and process until well combined.

Spoon evenly into the loaf pan and bake for 35–40 minutes or until a skewer comes out clean when inserted into the center of the cake. Leave in the pan for 5 minutes before turning out onto a wire rack. Warm the remaining honey in a saucepan over low heat for 1 minute or until runny. Brush the warm cake with the warm honey. Serve warm or cool.

Serves 8

Note: Alternatively, warm the honey in the microwave on medium-high for 30 seconds.
Variation: Fold ½ cup chopped walnuts or pecans through the mixture before transferring the mixture to the loaf pan.

Dried fruit and chocolate pillows

Cream cheese pastry
1/3 cup cream cheese, softened
1/4 cup superfine sugar
1 egg yolk
3 tablespoons milk
1 1/2 cups all-purpose flour
1 teaspoon baking powder
1 egg white, to glaze

Dried fruit filling
1/3 cup chopped dried figs
1/2 cup chopped dried apricots
1/2 cup raisins, chopped
2 oz. semisweet chocolate, chopped
1/2 teaspoon grated lemon zest
1/4 cup clear honey
large pinch ground allspice
large pinch ground cinnamon

To make the cream cheese pastry, beat the cheese and sugar until fluffy. Beat in the egg yolk and milk, then sift in the flour, a pinch of salt, and the baking powder, and form into a smooth dough. Cover with plastic wrap and refrigerate for 2 hours.

To make the dried fruit filling, put all the ingredients in a food processor and process in short bursts until finely chopped.

Preheat the oven to 350°F. Divide the fruit filling into three portions and roll into ropes, 13 inches long. Divide the pastry into three and, on a lightly floured surface, roll out to 13 x 4 inch rectangles.

Brush one length of a rectangle with water. Lay a portion of filling on the strip of pastry near the dry side. Roll the pastry over and press to seal, then cut into eight diagonal pieces and lay, seam-side down, on an ungreased cookie sheet. Repeat with the remaining pastry and filling.

Mix the egg white with 1 tablespoon of cold water and glaze the cookies, then bake for 13–15 minutes or until golden. Leave for 2–3 minutes, then cool on a wire rack.

Makes 24

Pistachio, yogurt, and cardamom cake

1 cup unsalted pistachio nuts
$\frac{1}{2}$ teaspoon ground cardamom
$\frac{2}{3}$ cup unsalted butter, chopped
1 $\frac{1}{2}$ cups self-rising flour
1 $\frac{1}{4}$ cups superfine sugar
3 eggs
$\frac{1}{2}$ cup plain yogurt
1 lime

Preheat the oven to 350°F. Grease an 8 inch round cake pan and line the bottom with waxed paper. Place the pistachios and cardamom in a food processor and pulse until just chopped. Add the butter, flour, and $\frac{3}{4}$ cup of the superfine sugar and pulse for 20 seconds or until crumbly. Add the combined eggs and yogurt and pulse for 10 seconds or until just combined. Spoon into the pan and smooth the surface.

Bake for 45–50 minutes or until a skewer comes out clean when inserted into the center of the cake.

To make the syrup, peel the zest off the lime with a vegetable peeler—remove any white pith from the zest. Place the remaining superfine sugar and $\frac{1}{3}$ cup plus 1 tablespoon water in a saucepan and stir over low heat until the sugar has dissolved. Bring to a boil, then add the lime zest and cook for 5 minutes. Strain and cool slightly. Pierce the cake with a few skewer holes and pour the hot syrup over the cooled cake.

Serves 8

Ginger panforte bars

1/3 cup all-purpose flour
1 tablespoon cocoa powder
1 teaspoon ground ginger
1/2 teaspoon ground cardamom
1 teaspoon ground cinnamon
3/4 cup dried figs, chopped
1/4 cup glacé ginger, chopped
1/4 cup glacé pineapple, chopped
1/4 cup glacé apricots, chopped
1/4 cup chopped candied citrus peel
1 cup blanched almonds, toasted
  (see page 390)
1/3 cup superfine sugar
1/4 cup honey

Preheat the oven to 315°F. Lightly grease a shallow, 3 x 10 inch baking pan and line with waxed paper, allowing paper to hang over at the two short ends.

Sift the flour, cocoa, ginger, and spices into a large bowl. Add the fruit and almonds.

Heat the superfine sugar, honey, and 2 teaspoons water in a small saucepan over low heat, stirring until it's melted and just comes to a boil. Pour onto the dry ingredients and mix well. Press the mixture into the pan and bake for 35–40 minutes or until just firm. Cool in the pan, then chill until firm. Cut into thin slices.

Makes 20 pieces

Honey picnic cake

1¼ cups sour cream
¾ cup firmly packed light brown
  sugar
1 egg
2 cups whole-wheat flour
1 teaspoon baking powder
3 tablespoons honey, warmed
½ cup pecans, chopped

Preheat the oven to 300°F. Grease a 9 x 5 inch loaf pan and line the bottom and the two long sides with waxed paper.

Blend the sour cream, sugar, and egg in a food processor until combined. Add the flour and baking powder and process until well blended. Add the honey and process until mixed. Add the nuts and process just long enough for them to mix through.

Spoon into the prepared pan and bake for 1 hour or until a skewer comes out clean when inserted into the center of the cake. Leave in the pan for 15 minutes before turning out onto a wire rack to cool.

Serves 8–10

Note: This cake is delicious served either as it is or with butter.

Lemon ricotta bars

1³/₄ cups all-purpose flour
1 teaspoon baking powder
³/₄ cup unsalted butter, melted
1 cup superfine sugar
4 eggs
1¹/₃ cups ricotta cheese
³/₄ cup whipping cream
2 tablespoons lemon zest
³/₄ cup lemon juice
confectioners' sugar, to dust

Preheat the oven to 350°F. Lightly grease a 12 x 8 inch baking pan and line with waxed paper, allowing paper to hang over the two long sides.

Put the flour, baking powder, butter, and half of the superfine sugar in a food processor and process in short bursts until the mixture comes together in a ball. Add one egg and process until combined.

Press the mixture into the pan. Bake for 15 minutes. Remove from the oven. Reduce the oven to 300°F.

Place the ricotta, cream, lemon zest and juice, the remaining sugar, and remaining eggs in the cleaned food processor and combine the ingredients for 1–2 seconds. Pour onto the pastry base and bake for 25–30 minutes—the topping will still have a slight wobble at this stage. Cool slightly, then refrigerate for 2 hours to firm. Cut into pieces. Dust with confectioners' sugar and serve.

Makes 15 pieces

Milk chocolate cupcakes

⅓ cup unsalted butter
2½ oz. milk chocolate, chopped
⅓ cup firmly packed brown sugar
2 eggs, lightly beaten
½ cup self-rising flour, sifted

Ganache
2¾ oz. milk chocolate, chopped
2 tablespoons heavy cream

Preheat the oven to 315°F. Line a flat-bottomed, twelve-cup standard muffin pan with paper liners. Put the butter and chocolate in a heatproof bowl and place over a saucepan of simmering water—make sure the bottom of the bowl doesn't touch the water. Stir until melted and combined. Remove the bowl from the heat, add the sugar and beaten eggs, and mix. Stir in the flour.

Transfer the mixture to a measuring cup and pour into the paper liners. Bake for 20–25 minutes or until cooked. Leave in the pan for 10 minutes, then transfer to a wire rack to cool.

To make the ganache, place the chocolate and cream in a heatproof bowl. Place over a saucepan of simmering water, making sure the bottom of the bowl doesn't touch the water. Once the chocolate has almost melted, remove the bowl from the heat and stir until the remaining chocolate has melted and the mixture is smooth. Allow to cool for about 8 minutes or until thickened slightly. Return the cakes to the cold muffin pan to keep them stable while you spread one heaping teaspoon of ganache over the top. If desired, decorate with sugar sprinkles.

Makes 12

Scottish shortbread

1 cup unsalted butter, softened
2/3 cup superfine sugar
1 2/3 cups all-purpose flour
1/2 cup rice flour
1 teaspoon sugar

Preheat the oven to 315°F. Brush an 11 inch round pizza pan with melted butter or oil and line with waxed paper.

Beat the butter and sugar with an electric mixer in a small bowl until light and creamy. Transfer to a large bowl and add the sifted flours. Mix to a soft dough with a flat-bladed knife. Lift the dough onto a lightly floured work surface and knead for 30 seconds or until smooth.

Transfer to the pizza pan and press into a 10 inch round (the pan must be larger than the uncooked shortbread, as the mixture will spread during cooking). Pinch and flute around the edge with your fingers to decorate. Prick the surface lightly with a fork and mark into sixteen segments with a sharp knife. Sprinkle with sugar and bake on the middle shelf of the oven for 35 minutes or until firm and pale golden. Allow the shortbread to cool in the pan.

Makes 16 pieces

Spiced Christmas muffins

1¾ cups mixed dried fruit
⅓ cup rum or brandy
2½ cups self-rising flour
1 teaspoon pumpkin pie spice
1 teaspoon ground cinnamon
½ teaspoon ground nutmeg
⅔ cup firmly packed light brown
  sugar
½ cup milk
1 egg, lightly beaten
2 tablespoons apricot preserves
½ teaspoon very finely grated
  lemon zest
½ teaspoon very finely grated
  orange zest
½ cup unsalted butter, melted
  and cooled
4 oz. store-bought icing
confectioners' sugar, to dust
2 tablespoons apricot preserves,
  extra, warmed and sieved
red and green glacé cherries, for
  decoration

Place the dried fruit and rum in a large bowl and mix together. Cover and soak, stirring often, for 1–2 hours.

Preheat the oven to 400°F. Line twelve muffin cups with paper liners. Sift the flour, pumpkin pie spice, cinnamon, and nutmeg into a large bowl and stir in the brown sugar. Make a well in the center.

Put the milk, egg, preserves, lemon and orange zest, and melted butter in a bowl, mix together, and pour into the well. Stir in the dried fruit mixture. Fold gently until just combined—the batter should be slightly lumpy.

Divide the mixture evenly among the muffin cups. Bake for 20 minutes or until a skewer inserted in the middle of the muffins comes out clean. Cool in the cups for 5 minutes, then transfer to a wire rack to cool completely.

Place the store-bought icing on a work surface dusted with a little confectioners' sugar. Roll out to ⅛ inch thick and, using a 3 inch, fluted round cutter, cut out twelve rounds. Brush the muffin tops with the extra preserves and top each with a round of icing. Decorate with whole or halved red glacé cherries and small "leaves" of green glacé cherries.

Makes 12 muffins

Butter almond torte

¹/₂ cup unsalted butter, chopped
¹/₃ cup milk
2 eggs
1 teaspoon vanilla extract
2 cups superfine sugar
1 cup all-purpose flour
2 teaspoons baking powder
³/₄ cup slivered almonds

Preheat the oven to 350°F. Line the bottom of a 9 inch springform pan with foil and lightly grease the bottom and side. Heat ¹/₄ cup of the butter and almost all of the milk in a small saucepan until the butter has melted.

Beat the eggs, vanilla, and ³/₄ cup of the sugar with an electric mixer until thick and creamy. Stir in the butter and milk mixture. Sift in almost all of the flour and all of the baking powder and stir to combine—the mixture will be thin. Pour into the pan and bake for 50 minutes.

Melt the remaining butter in a small saucepan. Stir in the almonds with the remaining sugar, flour, and milk and stir until combined. Quickly spoon the topping onto the cake (the center will still be uncooked), starting from the outside edges and avoid piling the topping in the center. Return to the oven for another 10–15 minutes or until golden and cooked through. Cool in the pan before inverting onto a wire rack.

Serves 8–10

Note: This torte is great served as a dessert with whipped cream.

Polenta cake

⅓ cup golden raisins
2 tablespoons brandy
1 cup ricotta cheese
1 cup superfine sugar
1½ cups polenta
pinch of grated nutmeg
½ teaspoon grated lemon zest
¼ teaspoon vanilla extract
1 tablespoon unsalted butter, chilled
    and cut into small cubes
2 tablespoons pine nuts
confectioners' sugar, to dust
heavy cream, to serve

Put the golden raisins and brandy in a small bowl with enough water to cover them and leave for 30 minutes. Drain and dry well on paper towels.

Preheat the oven to 315°F and grease a 10 inch loose-bottomed or springform cake pan with a tight-fitting bottom.

Put the ricotta in a large bowl and add 1¾ cups cold water. Beat with a wire whisk or electric mixer until smooth. Don't be alarmed by the thinness of the mixture—it can be very liquid, depending on the brand of ricotta used. Add the sugar and beat until smooth, then stir in the polenta, nutmeg, lemon zest, vanilla extract, and golden raisins.

Pour the mixture into the pan. Dot the surface with butter and sprinkle the pine nuts on top. Put the pan on a cookie sheet to catch any drips and bake for about 1 hour 30 minutes or until golden and set. Serve warm or cold, dusted with confectioners' sugar and accompanied with whipped cream.

Serves 8–10

Coffee cupcakes

3/4 cup unsalted butter, softened
2/3 cup light brown sugar
2 eggs
1 tablespoon strong coffee
1 1/4 cups self-rising flour
3/4 cup buttermilk
1 cup confectioners' sugar
1 teaspoon strong coffee, extra

Preheat the oven to 300°F. Line two twelve-cup tartlet pans with fluted paper liners. Beat all but 1/2 tablespoon of the butter and all the brown sugar with an electric mixer until light and creamy. Add the eggs one at a time, beating well after each addition. Mix in the tablespoon of coffee.

Fold the flour and a pinch of salt alternately with the buttermilk into the creamed mixture until combined. Spoon evenly into the paper liners and bake for 25–30 minutes or until just springy to the touch. Allow to cool in the pans.

To make the icing, combine the remaining butter, remaining coffee, the confectioners' sugar, and 1 1/2 tablespoons boiling water in a small bowl. Spread a little icing over each cupcake with a flexible bladed knife until evenly covered. If desired, decorate with chocolate-coated coffee beans.

Makes 24

Strawberry cheesecake muffins

1²/₃ cups strawberries, hulled
¹/₂ cup superfine sugar
¹/₃ cup cream cheese
1 tablespoon strawberry liqueur
1¹/₃ cups all-purpose flour
1 tablespoon baking powder
1 tablespoon butter, melted
1 teaspoon finely grated orange zest
1 egg
¹/₂ cup milk
confectioners' sugar, to dust

Preheat the oven to 350°F. Lightly grease six ¹/₂ cup nonstick muffin cups with oil. Set aside six small strawberries.

Place half the sugar in a bowl with the cream cheese and mix together well. Place the remaining strawberries in a blender or food processor with the strawberry liqueur and remaining sugar and blend until smooth. Pass through a fine strainer to remove the strawberry seeds.

Sift the flour and baking powder together in a large bowl and stir in the butter, orange zest, and ¹/₂ teaspoon salt. In a separate bowl, beat the egg and milk together, then add to the dry ingredients and mix well until combined. Do not overmix.

Spoon half of the mixture into the bottom of the muffin cups, then add a strawberry and a teaspoon of the cheese mixture. Top with the remaining muffin mixture and bake for 15 minutes or until cooked and golden. Remove muffins from the pans and cool slightly. Place a muffin on each serving plate, dust with confectioners' sugar, and serve drizzled with the sauce.

Makes 6

Desserts

Praline semifreddo

1¼ cups blanched almonds
1 cup superfine sugar
2½ cups heavy cream
2 eggs, separated
¾ cup confectioners' sugar, sifted
2 tablespoons Mandorla (almond-
flavored Marsala) or brandy

To make the praline, put the blanched almonds in a hot frying pan and dry-fry until well browned all over, then set aside. Melt the sugar in a saucepan over medium heat until golden, tipping the saucepan from side to side so the sugar melts evenly. Remove from the heat and stir in the almonds. Carefully pour into a greased baking tray and smooth out with the back of a spoon. Allow to cool completely, then finely crush the praline in a food processor. Pour the cream into a large bowl and whisk until soft peaks form.

Beat the egg yolks with a quarter of the confectioners' sugar until pale. Whisk the egg whites in a clean, dry glass bowl until firm peaks form, then gradually add the rest of the confectioners' sugar and whisk until glossy, firm peaks form. Gently fold the egg yolks into the cream, then fold in the egg whites. Fold in the praline and Mandorla.

Line six 1-cup metal dariole molds with two long strips of aluminum foil each, allowing the ends to hang over the edge. Spoon in the mixture, level the surface, and tap each mold on the counter. Cover with foil and freeze for 24 hours. To unmold, leave at room temperature for 5 minutes, then lift out with the foil.

Serves 6

Peaches cardinal

4 large ripe peaches
2½ cups raspberries
1 tablespoon confectioners' sugar,
  plus extra, to dust

If the peaches are very ripe, put them in a bowl and pour boiling water over them. Leave for a minute, then drain and carefully peel away the skin. If the fruit is not ripe enough, dissolve 2 tablespoons sugar in a saucepan of water, add the peaches, and cover the saucepan. Gently poach the peaches for 5–10 minutes or until they are tender. Drain and peel.

Let the peaches cool, then halve each one and remove the pit. Put two halves in each serving glass. Put the raspberries in a food processor or blender and mix until puréed (or mix by hand). Pass through a fine strainer to remove the seeds.

Sift the confectioners' sugar over the raspberry purée and stir in. Drizzle the purée over the peaches, cover, and chill thoroughly. Dust a little confectioners' sugar on top to serve.

Serves 4

Watermelon granita

1 lb. watermelon, skin and seeds
  removed
1 tablespoon superfine sugar
½ teaspoon lemon juice

Purée the watermelon in a blender or food processor, or chop it finely and push it through a metal strainer. Heat the sugar, lemon juice, and ⅓ cup water in a small saucepan for 4 minutes or until dissolved. Add the watermelon and stir well.

Pour into a plastic freezer box, cover, and freeze. Stir every 30 minutes with a fork during freezing to break up the ice crystals and give a better texture. Keep in the freezer until ready to serve, then roughly fork to break up the ice crystals.

Serves 4

Baked rice pudding

1 tablespoon unsalted butter, melted
3 tablespoons short-grain rice
3 eggs
1/4 cup superfine sugar
1 3/4 cups milk
1/2 cup whipping cream
1 teaspoon vanilla extract
1/4 teaspoon ground nutmeg

Preheat the oven to 315°F and brush a 6 cup flameproof dish with the melted butter. Cook the rice in a saucepan of boiling water for 12 minutes or until tender, then drain well.

Place the eggs in a bowl and beat lightly. Add the sugar, milk, cream, and vanilla extract and whisk until well combined. Stir in the cooked rice, pour into the prepared dish, and sprinkle with nutmeg.

Place the dish in a deep roasting pan and pour enough hot water into the pan to come halfway up the side of the dish. Bake for 45 minutes or until the custard is lightly set and a knife inserted into the center comes out clean. Remove the dish from the roasting pan and leave for 5 minutes before serving. Serve the pudding with poached or stewed fruit.

Serves 4–6

Variation: Add 2 tablespoons of golden raisins or chopped dried apricots to the custard mixture before baking.

Blueberry soy cheesecake

9 oz. graham crackers
3 teaspoons ground cinnamon
2/3 cup unsalted butter, melted
1 1/2 tablespoons powdered gelatin
9 oz. silken firm tofu
1/4 cup superfine sugar
1 cup cream cheese
10 oz. vanilla yogurt
2 cups blueberries, or 2 2/3 cups
    canned, well-drained blueberries, or
    2 cups frozen blueberries, thawed

Preheat the oven to 350°F. Grease a 9 inch springform pan.

Place the crackers and 1 teaspoon of the ground cinnamon in a food processor and blend together until it forms fine crumbs. Transfer to a bowl, add the melted butter, and mix well. Press the crumb mixture onto the base of the prepared pan. Bake for 10 minutes, then cool.

Pour 2/3 cup water into a heatproof bowl, evenly sprinkle on the gelatin, and leave until spongy—do not stir. Bring a saucepan of water to a boil and remove from the heat. Place the bowl of gelatin in the saucepan and stir until the gelatin is smooth.

Mix the tofu, sugar, cream cheese, and yogurt in a food processor until smooth. Add the gelatin and process in short bursts for 1–2 seconds.

Place the blueberries on the cracker base and pour the tofu mixture over the top, spreading evenly. Chill for at least 2 hours. Remove the side of the pan and dust the cheesecake with the remaining ground cinnamon just before serving.

Serves 6–8

Lemon delicious

¼ cup unsalted butter, at room
  temperature
¾ cup sugar
2 teaspoons finely grated lemon zest
3 eggs, separated
¼ cup self-rising flour
¾ cup milk
⅓ cup lemon juice
confectioners' sugar, to dust
heavy cream, to serve

Preheat the oven to 350°F. Melt
½ tablespoon of the butter and use
to lightly grease a 5 cup flameproof
ceramic dish.

Using an electric mixer, beat the
remaining butter, the sugar, and
grated zest together in a bowl until
the mixture is light and creamy.
Gradually add the egg yolks, beating
well after each addition. Fold in the
flour and milk alternately to make
a smooth but runny batter. Stir in
the lemon juice. Don't worry if the
batter looks like it has separated.

Whisk the egg whites in a clean, dry
bowl until firm peaks form, and, using
a large metal spoon, fold a third of
the whites into the batter. Gently fold
in the remaining egg whites, being
careful not to overmix.

Pour the batter into the prepared dish
and place in a large roasting pan.
Pour enough hot water into the pan to
come one-third of the way up the side
of the dish and bake for 55 minutes or
until the top of the pudding is golden,
risen, and firm to the touch. Leave
for 5 minutes before serving. Dust
with confectioners' sugar and serve
with whipped cream.

Serves 4–6

Baklava

2 1/4 cups superfine sugar
1 1/2 teaspoons lemon zest
1/4 cup honey
1/4 cup lemon juice
2 tablespoons orange blossom water
2 cups walnuts, finely chopped
1 1/3 cups shelled pistachios, finely
  chopped
1 1/3 cups almonds, finely chopped
2 tablespoons superfine sugar, extra
2 teaspoons ground cinnamon
13 oz. phyllo pastry
3/4 cup unsalted butter, melted

Put the sugar, lemon zest, and
1 1/2 cups water in a saucepan and
stir over high heat until the sugar
dissolves, then boil for 5 minutes.
Reduce the heat and simmer for
5 minutes. Add the honey, lemon
juice, and orange blossom water and
cook for 2 minutes. Remove from the
heat and refrigerate.

Preheat the oven to 325°F. Combine
the nuts, extra sugar, and cinnamon.
Grease a 13 x 11 inch baking dish.
Cover the bottom with a single layer
of phyllo pastry and brush lightly
with melted butter, folding in any
overhanging edges. Continue to layer
ten more sheets of the pastry in this
manner. Store the remaining pastry
under a damp dish towel.

Sprinkle half the nuts over the pastry
and pat down. Repeat the layering
and buttering of five more pastry
sheets, sprinkle with the rest of the
nuts, then layer and butter the
remaining pastry, brushing the top
with butter, and pat down. Score into
large diamonds. Pour any remaining
butter on top. Bake for 30 minutes,
then reduce the heat to 300°F and
cook for 30 minutes. Immediately
cut through the original diamond
markings, then strain the syrup over
the top. Refrigerate before serving.

Makes 18 pieces

White Christmas

1½ cups puffed rice cereal
1 cup milk powder
1 cup confectioners' sugar
1 cup dried shredded coconut
⅓ cup chopped red glacé cherries
⅓ cup chopped green glacé cherries
½ cup golden raisins
1 cup vegetable shortening

Line a shallow, 11 x 7 inch pan with aluminum foil. Put the puffed rice, milk powder, confectioners' sugar, coconut, glacé cherries, and golden raisins in a large bowl and stir. Make a well in the center.

Melt the shortening over low heat, cool slightly, then add to the well in the puffed rice mixture. Stir with a wooden spoon until all the ingredients are moistened.

Spoon the mixture into the prepared pan and smooth down the surface. Refrigerate for 30 minutes or until completely set. Remove from the pan, then peel away and discard the foil. Cut into small triangles to serve.

Makes 24 pieces

Chocolate rum mousse

9 oz. good-quality semisweet
  chocolate, chopped
3 eggs
¼ cup superfine sugar
2 teaspoons dark rum
1 cup heavy cream
heavy cream, extra, to serve
semisweet chocolate, extra, grated,
  to garnish

Put the chocolate in a heatproof bowl.
Half-fill a saucepan with water and
bring to a boil. Remove from the heat
and place the bowl over the pan,
making sure the bowl is not touching
the water. Stir occasionally until the
chocolate has melted. Allow to cool.

Using an electric mixer, beat the eggs
and sugar in a bowl for 5 minutes or
until the mixture is thick, pale, and
increased in volume. Transfer to a
large bowl.

Using a metal spoon, fold in the
melted chocolate with the rum, allow
the mixture to cool, then gently fold
in the lightly whipped cream until
just combined.

Spoon into four 1 cup ramekins
or dessert glasses. Refrigerate for
2 hours or until set. Serve with
extra whipped cream and garnish
with grated chocolate.

Serves 4

Passion fruit soufflé

superfine sugar, for lining ramekins
2 tablespoons unsalted butter
2 tablespoons all-purpose flour
3/4 cup milk
1/2 cup superfine sugar
1 cup fresh passion fruit pulp (about
    7 large passion fruit)
6 egg whites
confectioners' sugar, to dust

Preheat the oven to 350°F. Put a cookie sheet in the oven to heat. Lightly grease four 1 1/4 cup flameproof ramekins with oil and sprinkle the base and side of each with superfine sugar, shaking out any excess.

Melt the butter in a saucepan over medium heat, add the flour, and stir for 1 minute or until foaming. Remove from the heat and gradually add the milk. Return to the heat and stir constantly for 5–6 minutes or until the sauce boils and thickens. Reduce the heat and simmer, stirring, for 2 minutes. Transfer to a bowl and stir in the sugar and passion fruit pulp. Do not worry if the mixture looks curdled.

Using an electric mixer, beat the egg whites in a clean, dry bowl until firm peaks form. Using a metal spoon, fold a large dollop of the beaten egg whites into the passion fruit mixture, then gently fold in the remaining egg whites. Make sure you fold the mixture quickly and lightly to incorporate all of the egg whites without losing volume.

Spoon the mixture into the ramekins. Place on the cookie sheet and bake for 18–20 minutes or until golden and well risen but still a bit wobbly. Dust with confectioners' sugar and serve immediately.

Serves 4

Fruit poached in red wine

3 pears, peeled, quartered, and cored
3 apples, peeled, quartered, and
  cored
1/4 cup sugar
1 vanilla bean, cut in half lengthwise
2 small cinnamon sticks
1 2/3 cups red wine
3/4 cup dessert wine or port
1 lb. 9 oz. red-skinned plums, halved

Put the pears and apples in a large saucepan. Add the sugar, vanilla bean, cinnamon sticks, red wine, and dessert wine and bring to a boil. Reduce the heat and gently simmer for 5–10 minutes or until just soft.

Add the plums, stirring them through the pears and apples, and bring the syrup back to a simmer. Cook for another 5 minutes or until the plums are soft.

Remove the saucepan from the heat, cover with a lid, and allow the fruit to soak in the syrup for at least 6 hours. Reheat gently to serve warm, or serve at room temperature with whipped cream or ice cream and a cookie.

Serves 6

Mini éclairs

1/4 cup unsalted butter, chopped
1 cup all-purpose flour, sifted
4 eggs, beaten
1 1/4 cups heavy cream
1 tablespoon confectioners' sugar,
  sifted
1/2 teaspoon vanilla extract
2 oz. semisweet chocolate, melted
  (see page 390)

Preheat the oven to 400°F and line two cookie sheets with waxed paper. Put the butter in a saucepan with 1 cup water. Stir over low heat until melted. Bring to a boil, then remove from the heat and add all the flour. Beat with a wooden spoon until smooth. Return to the heat and beat for 2 minutes or until the mixture forms a ball and leaves the side of the saucepan. Remove from the heat and transfer to a bowl. Cool for 5 minutes. Add the beaten eggs, a little at a time, beating well between each addition, until thick and glossy—a wooden spoon should stand upright.

Spoon the mixture into a pastry bag with a 1/2 inch plain tip. Pipe 2 1/2 inch éclair shapes on the cookie sheets. Bake for 10 minutes, then reduce the heat to 350°F and bake for 10 minutes or until golden and puffed. Poke a hole into one side of each éclair and remove the soft dough from inside with a teaspoon. Return to the oven for 2–3 minutes. Cool on a rack.

Whip the cream, confectioners' sugar, and vanilla until thick. Pipe the cream into the side of each éclair. Dip the top of each éclair into the melted chocolate, then return to the wire rack for the chocolate to set.

Makes 24

Soy bavarois with mixed berries

2 egg yolks
1/4 cup superfine sugar
3/4 cup creamy soy milk
1 1/3 gelatin leaves
7 oz. soy berry yogurt, lightly beaten
1 cup mixed fresh or frozen berries
  (blackberries, strawberries,
  raspberries, blueberries)
1 tablespoon superfine sugar, extra

Lightly grease four 1/2 cup, metal dariole molds.

Combine the egg yolks and sugar in a flameproof bowl. Heat the milk in a saucepan over medium heat until almost boiling. Gradually pour onto the egg mixture, stirring constantly. Put the bowl over a saucepan of simmering water, ensuring the bowl doesn't touch the water, and stir for 10 minutes or until it thickens and coats the back of a spoon.

Soak the gelatin in cold water for 1 minute or until softened. Squeeze any excess water from the gelatin, add to the egg mixture, stirring until dissolved. Place the bowl over iced water to chill, and whisk frequently. When cool, gently whisk in the yogurt until thoroughly combined. Pour into the molds and refrigerate for at least 4 hours or until set.

Put the mixed berries in a saucepan with the extra sugar. Cook, stirring, over low heat for 3–5 minutes or until the sugar has dissolved. Allow to cool.

To serve, dip the dariole molds in hot water for 3–5 seconds and turn out onto serving plates. Spoon the mixed berries and syrup around the bavarois and serve.

Serves 4

Coffee granita

1 cup superfine sugar
5 cups very strong espresso coffee

Heat the superfine sugar with 2 tablespoons hot water in a saucepan until the sugar dissolves. Simmer for 3 minutes to make a syrup. Add the coffee and stir well.

Pour the mixture into a plastic or metal freezer box. The mixture should be no deeper than 1¼ inches so that the granita freezes quickly and breaks up easily. Stir every 2 hours with a fork to break up the ice crystals as they form. Repeat this two or three times. The granita is ready when almost set but still grainy. Stir a fork through it just before serving.

Serves 6

Rhubarb and berry crumble

1³/₄ lb. rhubarb, cut into 1 inch pieces
1¼ cups blackberries
1 teaspoon grated orange zest
1 cup superfine sugar
1 cup all-purpose flour
1 cup ground almonds
½ teaspoon ground ginger
²/₃ cup chilled unsalted butter, cubed

Preheat the oven to 350°F and grease a deep, 6 cup flameproof dish. Bring a saucepan of water to a boil over high heat, add the rhubarb, and cook for 2 minutes or until just tender. Drain well and combine with the berries, orange zest, and ⅓ cup of the superfine sugar. Taste and add a little more sugar if needed. Spoon the fruit mixture into the prepared dish.

To make the topping, combine the flour, ground almonds, ginger, and the remaining sugar. Cut the butter into the flour mixture with a pastry blender or rub in with your fingertips until it resembles coarse bread crumbs. Sprinkle the crumble mix over the fruit, pressing lightly. Don't press it down too firmly or it will become flat and dense.

Put the dish on a cookie sheet and bake for 25–30 minutes or until the topping is golden and the fruit is bubbling underneath. Leave for 5 minutes, then serve with whipped cream or ice cream.

Serves 4

Note: Substitute raspberries, loganberries, or blueberries for the blackberries. Strawberries do not work well, as they become too soft when cooked.

Mandarin ice

10 mandarin oranges
1/2 cup superfine sugar

Squeeze the mandarin oranges to make 2 cups juice, then strain.

Place the sugar and 1 cup water in a small saucepan. Stir over low heat until the sugar has dissolved, then simmer for 5 minutes. Remove from the heat and cool slightly.

Stir the mandarin juice into the sugar syrup, then pour into a shallow metal tray. Freeze for 2 hours or until frozen. Transfer to a food processor and blend until slushy. Return to the freezer and repeat the process three more times.

Serves 4–6

Cherry clafoutis

1 lb. fresh cherries (see Note)
³/₄ cup all-purpose flour
2 eggs, lightly beaten
¹/₃ cup superfine sugar
1 cup milk
¹/₄ cup heavy cream
¹/₄ cup unsalted butter, melted
confectioners' sugar, to dust

Preheat the oven to 350°F. Lightly brush a 6 cup flameproof dish with melted butter.

Carefully pit the cherries, then spread into the dish in a single layer.

Sift the flour into a bowl, add the egg, and whisk until smooth. Add the superfine sugar, milk, cream, and butter, whisking until just combined, but being careful not to overbeat.

Pour the batter over the cherries and bake for 30–40 minutes or until a skewer comes out clean when inserted into the center. Remove from the oven and dust generously with confectioners' sugar. Serve immediately.

Serves 6–8

Note: You can use a 20 oz. jar of cherries. Make sure you thoroughly drain the juice away.
Variation: Blueberries, blackberries, raspberries, or small, well-flavored strawberries can be used. A delicious version can be made using slices of poached pear.

Self-saucing chocolate pudding

½ tablespoon unsalted butter, melted
¼ cup unsalted butter, chopped,
   extra
2½ oz. good-quality semisweet
   chocolate, chopped
½ cup milk
1 cup self-rising flour
4 tablespoons cocoa powder
¾ cup superfine sugar
1 egg, lightly beaten
½ cup firmly packed light brown
   sugar
confectioners' sugar, to dust
whipped cream or ice cream,
   to serve

Preheat the oven to 350°F and lightly grease an 8 cup flameproof dish with the melted butter.

Place the chopped butter, chocolate, and milk in a small saucepan and stir over medium heat for 3–4 minutes or until the butter and chocolate have melted. Remove the saucepan from the heat and allow to cool slightly.

Sift the flour and 2 tablespoons of cocoa and add to the chocolate mixture with the superfine sugar and the egg, stirring until just combined. Spoon into the prepared dish.

Sift the remaining cocoa evenly over the top of the pudding and sprinkle with the brown sugar. Pour 2¼ cups boiling water over the back of a spoon (this keeps the water from making holes in the cake mixture) over the top of the pudding. Bake for 40 minutes or until the pudding is firm to the touch. Leave for 2 minutes before dusting with confectioners' sugar. Serve with whipped cream or ice cream.

Serves 6

Panna cotta

1³/₄ cups heavy cream
4 tablespoons superfine sugar
vanilla extract
1¼ teaspoons powdered gelatin
1 cup fresh berries

Put the cream and sugar in a saucepan and stir over gentle heat until the sugar has dissolved. Bring to a boil, then simmer for 3 minutes, adding a few drops of vanilla extract to taste.

Sprinkle the powdered gelatin onto the hot cream in an even layer and allow it to sponge for a minute, then stir it into the cream until dissolved.

Pour the cream mixture into four ½ cup metal dariole molds, cover each with plastic wrap, and refrigerate until set.

Unmold the panna cotta by wrapping the molds in a cloth dipped in hot water and tipping them gently onto individual plates. Serve with the fresh berries.

Serves 4

Sticky date puddings

1 cup dates, pitted and roughly
  chopped
1 teaspoon baking soda
$1/3$ cup unsalted butter, softened
$2/3$ cup firmly packed light brown
  sugar
1 teaspoon vanilla extract
2 eggs
$1 1/2$ cups self-rising flour, sifted
1 cup walnut halves, roughly chopped

Caramel sauce
$2/3$ cup firmly packed light brown
  sugar
$1/4$ cup unsalted butter
1 cup whipping cream

Preheat the oven to 350°F. Lightly brush six 1 cup molds with melted butter and line the bottoms with circles of waxed paper. Put the dates and baking soda in a saucepan and pour in 1 cup water. Bring to a boil, remove from the heat, and allow to cool (the mixture will become foamy).

Beat the butter, sugar, and vanilla with an electric mixer until light and creamy. Add 1 egg, beat well, and fold in 1 tablespoon of the flour. Add the other egg and repeat the process.

Fold through the remaining flour, walnuts, and date mixture and mix well. Divide the mixture among the molds, filling them three-quarters full. Bake for 30–35 minutes or until slightly risen and firm to the touch.

To make the caramel sauce, put the brown sugar, butter, and cream in a saucepan and simmer for 5 minutes. When the puddings are cooked, remove from the oven and prick a few holes in each one. Drizzle with some of the caramel sauce and return to the oven for 5 minutes. Loosen the side of each pudding with a small knife, turn out, remove the waxed paper, and serve with the remaining sauce.

Serves 6

Red fruit salad with berries

Syrup
1/4 cup superfine sugar
1/2 cup dry red wine
1 star anise
1 teaspoon finely chopped lemon zest

1 2/3 cups strawberries, hulled and
  halved
1 cup blueberries
1 1/4 cups raspberries, mulberries, or
  other red berries
1 1/4 cups cherries
5 small red plums, pits removed,
  quartered
yogurt, to serve

To make the syrup, place the sugar,
wine, star anise, lemon zest, and
1/2 cup water in a small saucepan.
Bring to a boil over medium heat,
stirring to dissolve the sugar. Boil the
syrup for 3 minutes, then set aside to
cool for 30 minutes. When cool, strain
the syrup.

Mix the fruit together in a large bowl
and pour in the red wine syrup. Mix
well to coat the fruit in the syrup and
refrigerate for 1 hour 30 minutes.
Serve the fruit dressed with a little
syrup and the yogurt.

Serves 6

Banana fritters in coconut batter

½ cup glutinous rice flour
1 cup freshly grated coconut or
 ⅔ cup dried shredded coconut
¼ cup sugar
1 tablespoon sesame seeds
¼ cup coconut milk
6 bananas
oil, for deep-frying
ice cream, to serve

Place the flour, coconut, sugar, sesame seeds, coconut milk, and ¼ cup water in a bowl and whisk to a smooth batter—add more water if the batter is too thick. Set aside to rest for 1 hour.

Peel the bananas and cut in half lengthwise (cut each portion in half crosswise if the bananas are large).

Fill a wok or deep, heavy-bottomed saucepan one-third full of oil and heat to 350°F or until a cube of bread browns in 15 seconds. Dip each piece of banana into the batter, then drop gently into the hot oil. Cook in batches for 4–6 minutes or until golden brown all over. Remove with a slotted spoon and drain on paper towels. Serve hot with ice cream.

Serves 6

Tipsy strawberry trifle

2 x 3 oz. packets strawberry-flavored
  gelatin powder
1 cup brandy or rum
1 cup milk
18 oz. thin sponge finger cookies
  (savoiardi)
1 lb. strawberries, hulled and sliced
3 cups store-bought custard sauce
1 1/4 cups heavy cream

Mix the gelatin powder with 1 3/4 cups boiling water and stir to dissolve. Pour into a shallow pan and refrigerate until the gelatin has just set but is not firm.

Combine the brandy and milk in a dish. Dip half the cookies in the brandy mixture, then place in a single layer in a 12-cup glass or ceramic dish. Spoon half the gelatin dessert over the cookies. Sprinkle with half the strawberries and then pour on half of the custard sauce.

Dip the remaining sponge fingers in the brandy mixture and place evenly over the custard, followed by most of the remaining gelatin and custard. Whip the cream and spread it evenly over the custard and top with the remaining strawberries and gelatin. Cover and refrigerate for 4 hours before serving.

Serves 8

Petits pots de crème

1²/₃ cups milk
1 vanilla bean
3 egg yolks
1 egg
¹/₃ cup superfine sugar

Preheat the oven to 275°F. Put the milk in a saucepan. Split the vanilla bean in two, scrape out the seeds, and add the bean halves and seeds to the milk. Bring the milk just to a boil.

Meanwhile, mix together the egg yolks, egg, and sugar. Strain the boiling milk over the egg mixture and stir well. Skim the surface to remove any foam.

Ladle the mixture into four ¹/₂ cup ramekins and place in a roasting pan. Pour enough hot water into the pan to come halfway up the sides of the ramekins. Bake for 30 minutes or until the custards are firm to the touch. Allow the ramekins to cool on a wire rack, then refrigerate until ready to serve.

Serves 4

Sticky black rice pudding

2 cups black rice
3 fresh pandan leaves
2 cups coconut milk
3 oz. palm sugar, grated
3 tablespoons superfine sugar
coconut cream, to serve
mango or papaya cubes, to serve

Place the rice in a large glass or ceramic bowl and cover with water. Allow to soak for at least 8 hours or preferably overnight. Drain, then place in a saucepan with 4 cups water and slowly bring to a boil. Cook at a low boil, stirring frequently, for 20 minutes or until tender. Drain.

Pull your fingers through the pandan leaves to shred them and then tie them in a knot. Pour the coconut milk into a large saucepan and heat until almost boiling. Add the palm sugar, superfine sugar, and pandan leaves and stir until the sugars have dissolved.

Add the rice to the saucepan and cook, stirring, for 8 minutes without boiling. Turn off the heat, cover, and set aside for 15 minutes while the rice absorbs the flavors. Remove the pandan leaves.

Spoon into bowls and serve warm with coconut cream and fresh mango.

Serves 6–8

Note: Black rice, pandan leaves, and palm sugar are available from Asian food stores. If palm sugar is unavailable, use light brown sugar.

Baked cheesecake

9 oz. butternut cookies
1 teaspoon pumpkin pie spice
$1/3$ cup butter, melted
2 cups cream cheese, softened
$3/4$ cup superfine sugar
4 eggs
1 teaspoon vanilla extract
1 tablespoon orange juice
1 tablespoon grated orange zest

Topping
1 cup sour cream
$1/2$ teaspoon vanilla extract
3 teaspoons orange juice
1 tablespoon superfine sugar
freshly grated nutmeg

Lightly grease the bottom of an 8 inch springform pan.

Finely crush the cookies in a food processor for 30 seconds or put them in a plastic bag and roll with a rolling pin. Transfer to a bowl and add the pumpkin pie spice and butter. Stir until all the crumbs are moistened, then spoon the mixture into the pan and press it firmly into the bottom and side. Refrigerate for 20 minutes or until firm.

Preheat the oven to 350°F. Beat the cream cheese until smooth. Add the sugar and beat until smooth. Add the eggs, one at a time, beating well after each addition. Mix in the vanilla, orange juice, and zest.

Pour the mixture into the crumb case and bake for 45 minutes or until just firm. To make the topping, combine the sour cream, vanilla, orange juice, and sugar in a bowl. Spread over the cheesecake, sprinkle with nutmeg, and return to the oven for 7 minutes. Cool, then refrigerate until firm.

Serves 8

Lemon gelato

5 egg yolks
½ cup sugar
2 cups milk
2 tablespoons grated lemon zest
¾ cup lemon juice
3 tablespoons heavy cream

Whisk the egg yolks and half the sugar together until pale and creamy. Put the milk, lemon zest, and remaining sugar in a saucepan and bring to a boil. Pour over the egg mixture and whisk to combine.

Pour the custard back into the saucepan and cook over low heat, stirring continuously until the mixture is thick enough to coat the back of a wooden spoon—do not allow the custard to boil. Strain the custard into a bowl, add the lemon juice and cream, then cool over ice.

Churn in an ice cream maker, following the manufacturer's instructions. Or, pour into a plastic freezer box, cover, and freeze. Stir every 30 minutes with a whisk during freezing to break up the ice crystals and give a better texture. Keep in the freezer until ready to serve.

Serves 6

Apple tapioca pudding

1/3 cup superfine sugar
1/2 cup tapioca
2 1/2 cups milk
1/2 cup golden raisins
1 teaspoon vanilla extract
pinch ground nutmeg
1/4 teaspoon ground cinnamon
2 eggs, lightly beaten
3 small ripe apples, peeled, cored,
    and very thinly sliced
1 tablespoon light brown sugar

Preheat the oven to 350°F. Grease a 6 cup ceramic soufflé dish. Place the sugar, tapioca, milk, golden raisins, and 1/4 teaspoon salt in a saucepan and heat, stirring often. Bring to a boil, then reduce the heat and simmer for 5 minutes.

Stir in the vanilla extract, nutmeg, cinnamon, egg, and the apple slices, then pour into the prepared dish. Sprinkle with the brown sugar and bake for 45 minutes or until set and golden brown.

Serves 4

Passion fruit mousse

6 passion fruit
6 eggs, separated
3/4 cup superfine sugar
1/2 teaspoon finely grated lemon zest
3 tablespoons lemon juice
1 tablespoon powdered gelatin
1 1/4 cups heavy cream, lightly
  whipped
3/4 cup flaked or 2/3 cup shredded
  coconut, toasted

Cut the passion fruit in half and scoop out the pulp. Strain, then measure out 3 tablespoons of juice and set aside. Add the seeds and pulp to the remaining juice and set aside. Put the egg yolks, 1/2 cup of the sugar, lemon zest, lemon juice, and strained passion fruit juice in a heatproof bowl. Put the bowl over a saucepan of simmering water and, using an electric mixer, beat for 10 minutes or until thick and creamy. Remove from the heat and transfer to a glass bowl.

Sprinkle the gelatin over 1/2 cup water in a small bowl and leave until spongy. Put the bowl in a saucepan of just-boiled water (the water should come halfway up the bowl) and stir until dissolved. Add the gelatin to the mousse mixture and mix well. Mix in the passion fruit pulp and leave until cold, then fold in the whipped cream.

Using an electric mixer, whisk the egg whites until soft peaks form. Gradually whisk in the remaining sugar, beating until the sugar has dissolved. Fold the egg whites into the mousse mixture quickly and lightly. Spoon into eight 1 cup ramekins or stemmed wine glasses. Refrigerate for 2 hours or until set. Sprinkle with the coconut just before serving.

Serves 10–12

Plum cobbler

1³/₄ lb. can dark plums, pitted
1 tablespoon honey
2 ripe pears, peeled, cored, and cut
    into eighths

Topping
1 cup self-rising flour
1 tablespoon superfine sugar
¹/₄ teaspoon ground cardamom or
    ground cinnamon
2 tablespoons unsalted butter, chilled
    and chopped
¹/₄ cup milk
extra milk, for brushing
1 tablespoon superfine sugar, extra
¹/₄ teaspoon ground cardamom or
    ground cinnamon, extra

Preheat the oven to 400°F. Grease a round, 7 inch, flameproof dish. Drain the plums, reserving ³/₄ cup of the syrup. Place the syrup, honey, and pear in a large, wide saucepan and bring to a boil. Reduce the heat and simmer for 8 minutes or until the pear is tender. Add the plums.

To make the topping, sift the flour, sugar, cardamom, and a pinch of salt into a large bowl. Cut in the butter with a pastry blender or rub in with your fingers until the mixture resembles fine bread crumbs. Stir in the milk using a flat-bladed knife, mixing lightly to form a soft dough. Add a little more milk if necessary. Turn onto a lightly floured surface and form into a smooth ball. Roll out to a ¹/₂ inch thickness and cut into rounds with a 1¹/₂ inch cutter.

Spoon the hot fruit into the dish, then arrange the circles of dough in an overlapping pattern over the fruit on the inside edge of the dish only—leave the fruit in the center exposed. Brush the dough with the extra milk. Mix the extra sugar and cardamom and sprinkle over the dough.

Place the dish on a cookie sheet and bake for 30 minutes or until the topping is golden and cooked.

Serves 4

Cinnamon orange mini pavlovas with berries

2 egg whites
½ cup superfine sugar
2 teaspoons ground cinnamon
1 teaspoon finely grated orange zest
3 teaspoons cornstarch
1 teaspoon white vinegar
½ cup heavy cream
fresh berries

Preheat the oven to 275°F. Line a cookie sheet with waxed paper and mark four 4 inch circles. Turn the waxed paper upside down so the marks don't stain the meringue.

Beat the egg whites with an electric mixer until soft peaks form. Gradually add the sugar, beating well after each addition. Continue to beat for 4–5 minutes or until the sugar has dissolved and the meringue is thick and glossy. Gently fold in the cinnamon, orange zest, cornstarch, and vinegar. Place 2 tablespoons of the mixture into each circle, gently spreading it out to the edges with the back of a spoon. Hollow out each center to make nest shapes.

Bake for 10 minutes, then turn the cookie sheet around and bake for another 30–35 minutes or until the pavlovas are pale and crisp. Turn the oven off and allow them to cool completely with the door slightly ajar. The pavlovas may crack slightly on cooling. Whip the cream and spoon a little into each pavlova, top with the berries, and serve immediately.

Serves 4

Zabaglione

6 egg yolks
3 tablespoons superfine sugar
½ cup sweet Marsala
1 cup heavy cream

Whisk the egg yolks and sugar in the top of a double boiler or in a heatproof bowl set over a saucepan of simmering water. Make sure that the water does not touch the bottom of the bowl or the egg may overcook and stick. It is important that you whisk constantly to move the cooked mixture from the outside of the bowl to the center.

When the egg mixture is tepid, add the Marsala and whisk for another 5 minutes or until it has thickened enough to hold its shape when drizzled off the whisk into the bowl.

Whip the cream until soft peaks form. Gently fold in the egg and Marsala mixture. Divide among four glasses or bowls. Cover and refrigerate for 3–4 hours before serving.

Serves 4

Bread and butter pudding

2 tablespoons golden raisins
1 tablespoon Grand Marnier
10 slices day-old white bread, crusts
  removed
2½ tablespoons marmalade or
  apricot preserves
2 eggs
2 tablespoons superfine sugar
2 cups milk
1 teaspoon vanilla extract

Place the golden raisins in a bowl, add the Grand Marnier, toss to coat, and leave for 30 minutes. Preheat the oven to 315°F.

Spread the slices of bread with 1½ tablespoons of the marmalade. Cut each slice into four triangles. Lightly grease a 6 cup flameproof dish with oil. Layer the bread in the dish, sprinkling the golden raisins between the layers.

Whisk the eggs, sugar, milk, and vanilla extract together in a bowl. Pour over the bread and allow to soak for at least 30 minutes.

Place the dish in a large roasting pan and pour in boiling water to come halfway up the side of the dish, then bake in the oven for 35–40 minutes. Remove the dish from the roasting pan and brush with the remaining marmalade. Leave for 10 minutes, then serve.

Serves 6

Amaretti-stuffed peaches

6 ripe peaches
2 oz. amaretti cookies, crushed
1 egg yolk
2 tablespoons superfine sugar
¼ cup ground almonds
1 tablespoon amaretto
¼ cup white wine
1 teaspoon superfine sugar, extra
1 tablespoon unsalted butter

Preheat the oven to 350°F and lightly grease a 12 x 10 inch flameproof dish with butter.

Cut each peach in half and carefully remove the pits. Scoop a little of the pulp out from each and combine in a small bowl with the crushed cookies, egg yolk, superfine sugar, ground almonds, and amaretto.

Spoon some of the mixture into each peach and place them cut-side up in the dish. Sprinkle with the white wine and the extra sugar. Put a dot of butter on the top of each and bake for 20–25 minutes or until golden.

Serves 6

Note: When they are in season, you can also use ripe apricots or nectarines in this recipe.

Apricot honey soufflé

1 cup dried apricots, chopped
2 tablespoons superfine sugar
2 egg yolks
1½ tablespoons honey, warmed
1 teaspoon finely grated lemon zest
4 egg whites
confectioners' sugar, to dust

Place the apricots in a saucepan with ½ cup cold water, or enough to cover. Bring to a boil, then reduce the heat and simmer for 20 minutes or until the apricots are soft and pulpy. Drain, then process in a food processor to a purée.

Preheat the oven to 400°F. Lightly grease a 6 cup soufflé dish and sprinkle the bottom and side with 1 tablespoon of superfine sugar. Put the egg yolks, honey, zest, and apricot purée in a bowl and beat until smooth.

Whisk the egg whites in a clean, dry bowl until soft peaks form, then whisk in the remaining sugar. Fold 1 tablespoon into the apricot mixture and mix well. Lightly fold in the remaining egg white, being careful to keep the mixture light and aerated. Spoon into the soufflé dish and level the surface. Run your thumb around the inside rim to create a gap between the mixture and the wall of the dish (this will encourage even rising).

Bake on the upper shelf in the oven for 25–30 minutes or until risen and just set. Cover loosely with aluminum foil if the surface starts to overbrown. Dust with confectioners' sugar and serve.

Serves 4

Nougat

2 cups sugar
1 cup corn syrup
½ cup honey
2 egg whites
1 teaspoon vanilla extract
½ cup unsalted butter, softened
⅓ cup almonds, unblanched and
  toasted
½ cup glacé cherries (not imitation)

Grease an 11 x 7 inch baking dish and line with waxed paper. Place the sugar, syrup, honey, ¼ cup water, and ¼ teaspoon salt in a heavy-bottomed saucepan and stir over low heat until dissolved. Boil for 8 minutes or until the mixture reaches hard ball stage (see page 393) or 250°F on the sugar thermometer.

Beat the egg whites in a bowl with an electric mixer until firm peaks form. Slowly pour a quarter of the syrup onto the egg whites in a thin stream and beat for up to 5 minutes or until the mixture holds its shape. Place the remaining syrup over the heat and cook for 2 minutes or until it reaches hard crack stage (see page 393) or 290°F on the thermometer. Pour slowly onto the meringue mixture with the mixer running and beat until very thick.

Add the vanilla and butter and beat for 5 minutes. Stir in the almonds and cherries using a metal spoon. Turn the mixture into the pan and smooth the top with a flexible-bladed knife. Refrigerate for at least 4 hours or until firm. Cut into pieces with a very sharp knife. Wrap each piece in plastic wrap and store in the refrigerator.

Makes 2 lb.

Grilled figs with ricotta

2 tablespoons honey
1 cinnamon stick
3 tablespoons sliced almonds
4 large (or 8 small) fresh figs
$\frac{1}{2}$ cup ricotta cheese
$\frac{1}{2}$ teaspoon vanilla extract
2 tablespoons confectioners' sugar,
   sifted
pinch ground cinnamon
$\frac{1}{2}$ teaspoon finely grated orange zest

Place the honey and cinnamon stick in a small saucepan with $\frac{1}{3}$ cup water. Bring to a boil, then reduce the heat and simmer gently for 6 minutes or until thickened and reduced by half. Discard the cinnamon stick and stir in the almonds.

Preheat the broiler and grease a shallow, flameproof dish large enough to fit all the figs side by side. Slice the figs into quarters from the top to within $\frac{1}{2}$ inch of the bottom, keeping them attached at the base. Arrange in the prepared dish.

Mix the ricotta, vanilla, confectioners' sugar, ground cinnamon, and orange zest in a small bowl. Divide the filling among the figs, spooning it into their cavities. Spoon the syrup over the top. Place under the broiler and cook until the juices start to come out from the figs and the almonds are lightly toasted. Cool for 2–3 minutes. Spoon the juices and any fallen almonds from the bottom of the dish over the figs and serve.

Serves 4

Baked custard

½ tablespoon unsalted butter, melted
3 eggs
⅓ cup superfine sugar
2 cups milk
½ cup whipping cream
1½ teaspoons vanilla extract
ground nutmeg

Preheat the oven to 315°F and brush four 1 cup ramekins or a 6 cup flameproof dish with the melted butter.

Whisk together the eggs and sugar in a large bowl until they are combined. Place the milk and cream in a small saucepan and stir over medium heat for 3–4 minutes or until the mixture is warmed through, then stir into the egg mixture with the vanilla extract. Strain into the prepared dishes and sprinkle with the ground nutmeg.

Place the dishes in a deep roasting pan and add enough hot water to come halfway up the sides of the dishes. Bake for 25 minutes for the individual custards, 30 minutes for the large custard, or until it is set and a knife inserted into the center comes out clean.

Remove the custards from the roasting pan and leave for 10 minutes before serving.

Serves 4

Variation: Omit the vanilla and add 1½ tablespoons of Amaretto or Grand Marnier liqueur to the custard before baking.

Crème caramel

1 cup milk
1 cup whipping cream
1½ cups superfine sugar
1 teaspoon vanilla extract
4 eggs, lightly beaten
⅓ cup superfine sugar, extra

Preheat the oven to 400°F. Place the milk and cream in a saucepan and gradually bring to a boil.

Put the sugar in a frying pan and cook over medium heat for 8–10 minutes. Stir occasionally as the sugar melts to form a golden toffee. The sugar may become lumpy—break up any lumps with a wooden spoon. Pour the toffee into the bottom of six ½ cup ramekins or flameproof dishes.

Combine the vanilla, eggs, and extra sugar in a bowl. Remove the milk and cream from the heat and gradually add to the egg mixture, whisking well. Pour the custard mixture evenly over the toffee. Place the ramekins in a baking dish and pour in boiling water until it comes halfway up the sides of the dishes. Bake for 20 minutes or until set. Use a flat-bladed knife to run around the edges of the dishes and carefully turn out the crème caramel onto a serving plate, toffee side up.

Serves 6

Note: When making toffee, watch it carefully. It will take a little while to start melting, but once it starts, it will happen very quickly. Stir occasionally to make sure it melts evenly and doesn't stick to the saucepan.

Chocolate fudge pudding

2/3 cup unsalted butter
3/4 cup superfine sugar
3 1/2 oz. semisweet chocolate, melted
  and cooled (see page 390)
2 eggs
1/2 cup all-purpose flour
1 cup self-rising flour
1/4 cup cocoa powder
1 teaspoon baking soda
1/2 cup milk

Sauce
1/4 cup unsalted butter, chopped
4 oz. semisweet chocolate, chopped
1/2 cup whipping cream
1 teaspoon vanilla extract

Preheat the oven to 350°F. Lightly grease eight 1 cup metal molds with melted butter and line each bottom with a round of waxed paper.

Beat the butter and superfine sugar until light and creamy. Add the melted chocolate, beating well. Add the eggs one at a time, beating well after each addition.

Sift together the flours, cocoa powder, and baking soda, then fold into the chocolate mixture. Add the milk and fold through. Half-fill the molds. Cover the molds with pieces of greased aluminum foil and place in a large, deep baking dish. Pour in enough boiling water to come halfway up the sides of the molds. Bake for 35–40 minutes or until a skewer inserted into the center of each pudding comes out clean.

To make the sauce, combine the butter, chocolate, cream, and vanilla in a saucepan. Stir over low heat until the butter and chocolate have completely melted. Pour over the pudding and serve with whipped cream.

Serves 8

Crepes with warm fruit compote

Crepes
½ cup all-purpose flour
2 eggs
1 cup milk
2 teaspoons superfine sugar

Compote
½ cup whole dried apricots
¼ cup port or Muscat
1 vanilla bean, halved
2 firm pears, peeled, cored, and
   quartered
2 cinnamon sticks
15 oz. can pitted prunes in syrup,
   drained, syrup reserved

Place the flour in a bowl and gradually add the combined eggs and milk, whisking to remove any lumps. Cover the batter with plastic wrap and leave for 30 minutes.

To make the compote, put the apricots and port in a saucepan and cook, covered, over low heat for 2–3 minutes or until softened. Scrape the seeds from the vanilla bean and add both the seeds and vanilla bean to the saucepan along with the pears, cinnamon, and prune syrup. Simmer, covered, stirring occasionally, for 4 minutes or until the pears have softened. Add the prunes and simmer for 1 minute.

Heat an 8 inch, nonstick crepe pan or frying pan over medium heat. Lightly grease with oil. Pour ¼ cup of batter into the pan and swirl evenly over the bottom. Cook each crepe for 1 minute or until the underside is golden. Turn it over and cook the other side for 30 seconds, then remove. Keep warm and repeat to make eight crepes.

Fold the crepes into triangles and sprinkle with superfine sugar. Serve with the compote.

Serves 4

Apricots in cardamom syrup

1²/₃ cups dried apricots
3 tablespoons superfine sugar
3 tablespoons slivered, blanched
  almonds
¹/₂ inch piece of ginger, sliced
4 cardamom pods
1 cinnamon stick
4 pieces edible silver leaf (varak),
  optional

Soak the apricots in 3 cups water in a large saucepan for 4 hours or until plumped up.

Add the superfine sugar, almonds, ginger, cardamom pods, and cinnamon to the apricots and bring slowly to a boil, stirring until the sugar has dissolved. Reduce the heat to a simmer and cook until the liquid has reduced by half and formed a thick syrup. Pour into a bowl, then refrigerate.

Serve in small bowls with a piece of silver leaf (available in Indian food stores) for decoration. To do this, invert the piece of backing paper over each bowl. As soon as the silver leaf touches the apricots it will come away from the backing and stick to them.

Serves 4

Zuppa Inglese

Custard
6 large egg yolks
1/2 cup superfine sugar
2 tablespoons cornstarch
1 tablespoon all-purpose flour
2 1/2 cups milk
1/2 vanilla bean or 1 teaspoon vanilla
    extract

1 store-bought sponge cake
2/3 cup clear alcohol, such as grappa
    or kirsch
1 2/3 cups raspberries
3 cups blackberries
2 teaspoons superfine sugar
1 cup heavy cream

To make the custard, whisk the egg yolks with the sugar until pale and fluffy. Add the cornstarch and flour and mix well. Heat the milk with the vanilla bean and bring just to a boil. Pour into the egg mixture, whisking as you do so. Pour back into the saucepan and gently bring to a boil, stirring all the time. Once the mixture is just boiling, take it off the heat and stir for another few minutes. Pour into a bowl and cover the surface with plastic wrap to keep a skin from forming.

Slice the sponge cake into 3/4 inch strips. Place a couple of pieces on each plate (you need to use deep plates) and brush with about two-thirds of the alcohol. Allow to soak for at least 10 minutes.

Put the raspberries and blackberries in a saucepan with the remaining alcohol and the superfine sugar. Gently warm through so that the sugar just melts, then set aside to cool. Spoon over the sponge cake, then pour the custard over the top of the fruit. Lightly whip the cream and serve on the side.

Serves 6

Caramelized apple mousse

¼ cup unsalted butter
¼ cup superfine sugar
²/₃ cup heavy cream
1 lb. green apples, peeled, cored,
    and cut into thin wedges
2 eggs, separated

Place the butter and sugar in a frying pan and stir over low heat until the sugar has dissolved. Increase the heat to medium and cook until the mixture turns deeply golden, stirring frequently. Add 2 tablespoons of the cream and stir to remelt the caramel.

Add the apple wedges and cook, stirring frequently, over medium heat for 10–15 minutes or until caramelized. Remove eight apple wedges and set aside to use as garnish.

Blend the remaining apples and caramel in a food processor until smooth. Transfer to a large bowl, then stir in the egg yolks and allow to cool.

Whisk the egg whites in a clean, dry bowl until soft peaks form, then fold into the cooled apple mixture. Whip the remaining cream until firm peaks form and fold into the apple mixture. Pour into a 3 cup serving bowl or four ¾ cup individual serving molds. Refrigerate for 3 hours or until firm. Serve with the reserved apple wedges.

Serves 4

Caramel ice cream

⅓ cup sugar
⅓ cup whipping cream
3 egg yolks
1½ cups milk
1 vanilla bean

To make the caramel, put slightly more than half the sugar in a heavy-bottomed saucepan and heat until it dissolves and starts to caramelize—swirl the saucepan from side to side as the sugar cooks to keep the coloring even. Remove from the heat and carefully add the cream (it will splutter). Stir over low heat until the caramel remelts.

Whisk the egg yolks and remaining sugar until light and fluffy. Put the milk and vanilla bean in a saucepan and bring just to a boil, then strain over the caramel. Bring back to a boil and pour over the egg yolk mixture, whisking continuously.

Pour the custard back into the saucepan and cook, stirring, until it is thick enough to coat the back of a wooden spoon. Do not let it boil or it will split. Pass through a strainer into a bowl and set the bowl over ice to cool quickly.

Churn in an ice cream maker following the manufacturer's instructions. Or, pour into a plastic freezer box, cover, and freeze. Stir every 30 minutes with a whisk during freezing to break up the ice crystals. Freeze overnight with a layer of plastic wrap over the surface and the lid on the container. Keep in the freezer until ready to serve.

Serves 4

White chocolate mini cheesecakes with mixed berries

4 butternut cookies
1/2 cup good-quality white chocolate chips
1 cup cream cheese, at room temperature
1/4 cup heavy cream
1/2 cup superfine sugar
1 egg
1 1/2–2 cups mixed berries, such as raspberries, blueberries, and sliced strawberries
Framboise or Cointreau, optional

Preheat the oven to 315°F. Grease four jumbo muffin cups and line with two strips of waxed paper to make a cross pattern. Put a cookie in the bottom of each cup. Put the chocolate chips in a flameproof bowl. Bring a saucepan of water to a boil, then remove from the heat. Sit the bowl over the saucepan, making sure the bottom of the bowl does not sit in the water. Stir occasionally until the chocolate has melted.

Using an electric mixer, beat the cream cheese, cream, and half the sugar until thick and smooth. Beat in the egg and then the melted chocolate. Pour evenly into the muffin cups and bake for 25 minutes or until set. Cool completely in the pan, then carefully run a small spatula or flat-bladed knife around the edge and lift out of the cups using the paper strips as handles. Refrigerate for 1 hour or until ready to serve.

Place the berries in a bowl and fold in the remaining sugar. Leave for 10–15 minutes or until juices form. Flavor with a little liqueur, such as Framboise or Cointreau, if desired. Serve the cheesecakes on individual serving plates topped with the berries.

Serves 4

Cinnamon gelato

1 vanilla bean
2¼ cups heavy cream
2¼ cups milk
2 cinnamon sticks
6 egg yolks
½ cup superfine sugar

Split the vanilla bean down the middle, leaving it joined at one end, and put it in a saucepan with the cream, milk, and cinnamon sticks. Bring just to a boil, then remove from the heat and allow to infuse for 1 hour.

Whisk the egg yolks and sugar in a large bowl until pale and creamy. Pour the milk over the egg yolk mixture and whisk quickly to combine. Pour the custard back into the saucepan and cook over very low heat to just thicken it, stirring continuously with a wooden spoon. Remove from the heat and dip the spoon into the custard. Draw a line on the back of the spoon—if the line stays and the custard does not run through it, then it is ready; if not, cook a little longer. Do not allow the custard to boil.

Scrape out the vanilla seeds and mix them into the custard. Strain into a bowl, removing the vanilla bean and cinnamon sticks, and allow to cool. Churn in an ice cream maker following the manufacturer's instructions. Or, pour into a metal or plastic freezer box and freeze, whisking every 30 minutes to break up the ice crystals and give a creamy texture. Once set, keep in the freezer until ready to serve.

Serves 8

Coffee crémets with chocolate sauce

1 cup cream cheese
1 cup heavy cream
4 tablespoons very strong coffee
⅓ cup superfine sugar

Chocolate sauce
3½ oz. dark chocolate
¼ cup unsalted butter

Line four ½ cup ramekins or heart-shaped molds with cheesecloth, leaving enough cheesecloth hanging over the side to wrap over the crémet.

Beat the cream cheese a little until smooth, then whisk in the cream. Add the coffee and sugar and mix. Spoon into the ramekins and fold the cheesecloth over the top. Refrigerate for at least 1 hour 30 minutes, then unwrap the cheesecloth and turn the crémets out onto individual plates, carefully peeling the cheesecloth off each one.

To make the chocolate sauce, gently melt the chocolate in a saucepan with the butter and 4 tablespoons water. Stir well to make a shiny sauce, then let the sauce cool a little. Pour a little chocolate sauce over each crémet.

Serves 4

Note: Dark chocolate is available with different amounts of added sugar. For a really good chocolate sauce, use chocolate with less sugar and more cocoa solids (between 50 and 70 percent).

Pistachio crème brûlée

2 cups cream
1/4 cup finely chopped pistachios
1/2 vanilla bean, halved lengthwise
1/2 teaspoon grated orange zest
1/2 cup superfine sugar
5 egg yolks
1–3 tablespoons superfine sugar,
  extra
pistachio biscotti, to serve

Preheat the oven to 275°F. Put the cream, pistachios, vanilla bean, zest, and half the sugar in a saucepan over medium heat and stir to dissolve the sugar, then slowly bring to a boil. Remove from the heat and infuse for 10 minutes.

Whisk the egg yolks and remaining sugar in a bowl. Strain the cream mixture into a bowl, then add to the egg mixture, stirring continuously. Ladle the custard into six 1/2 cup ramekins and place in a roasting pan. Pour in cold water to come halfway up the sides of the ramekins, then place in the oven and cook for 1 hour or until the custard has set and is only just wobbly. Cool the ramekins on a wire rack, then refrigerate for 4 hours.

Preheat the broiler. Sprinkle 1–2 teaspoons of the extra sugar over the top of each brûlée. Put the brûlées in a roasting pan full of ice, then put the pan under the broiler for 4 minutes or until the tops of the brûlées have melted and caramelized. Remove the ramekins from the roasting pan and dry around the outside edges. Refrigerate for 1–2 hours, but not more than 3 hours or the toffee will start to go sticky and lose its crunch. Serve with pistachio biscotti and some fresh fruit.

Serves 6

Pies & Tarts

Chocolate and peanut butter pie

7 oz. chocolate cookies, crushed
1/4 cup unsalted butter, melted
3/4 cup cream cheese
2/3 cup confectioners' sugar, sifted
2/3 cup smooth peanut butter
1 teaspoon vanilla extract
1 cup heavy cream, whipped to
  firm peaks
1/4 cup whipping cream, extra
3 teaspoons unsalted butter, extra
1 3/4 oz. semisweet chocolate, grated
honey-roasted peanuts, chopped,
  to garnish

Combine the cookie crumbs with the melted butter and press into the bottom and side of a 9 inch (top) x 7 inch (bottom) x 1 1/4 inch (deep) pie dish and refrigerate for 15 minutes or until firm.

Put the cream cheese and confectioners' sugar in a bowl and beat with an electric mixer until smooth. Add the peanut butter and vanilla and beat together. Stir in a third of the whipped cream until smooth, then gently fold in the remaining whipped cream. Pour the mixture into the pie shell. Refrigerate for 2 hours or until firm.

Place the extra cream and butter in a saucepan and stir over medium heat until the butter is melted and the cream just comes to a simmer. Remove from the heat, add the grated chocolate, and stir until melted. Cool a little, then dribble the chocolate over the top of the pie to create a lattice pattern. Refrigerate for 2 hours or until the topping and chocolate are firm.

Remove the pie from the refrigerator, sprinkle with the chopped peanuts, and serve.

Serves 10–12

Lemon and passion fruit tarts with raspberries

¼ cup unsalted butter
⅓ cup superfine sugar
2 eggs
2 tablespoons self-rising flour, sifted
¼ cup lemon juice
1 teaspoon grated lemon zest
1 passion fruit, pulp removed
3 sheets phyllo pastry
1 cup fresh raspberries

Preheat the oven to 350°F. Beat the butter and superfine sugar until light and creamy. Add the eggs one at a time, beating well after each addition. Add the flour, lemon juice, zest, and passion fruit pulp and beat until well combined.

Fold each sheet of phyllo pastry in half from the short end up. Fold again and cut in half. Carefully line six standard muffin cups with a piece of pastry. Pour in the lemon mixture and bake for 20–25 minutes or until set.

Serve topped with fresh raspberries and, if desired, whipped cream.

Makes 6

Freeform blueberry pie

Crust

1 1/2 cups all-purpose flour
1/3 cup unsalted butter, chilled and
  cubed
2 teaspoons grated orange zest
1 tablespoon superfine sugar
2–3 tablespoons ice water

1/3 cup crushed amaretti cookies or
  almond bread
1/2 cup all-purpose flour
1 teaspoon ground cinnamon
1/3 cup superfine sugar
3 1/4 cups fresh blueberries
milk, for brushing
2 tablespoons blueberry preserves
confectioners' sugar, to dust

Sift the flour into a large bowl and rub in the butter with your fingertips until the mixture resembles bread crumbs. Stir in the orange zest and sugar. Make a well, add almost all the water, and mix with a flat-bladed knife, using a cutting action, until the mixture comes together in beads. Add a little more water if necessary to bring the dough together. Gather together and lift out onto a lightly floured surface. Press together into a ball and flatten it slightly into a disk. Cover in plastic wrap and refrigerate for 20 minutes.

Preheat the oven to 400°F. Combine the crushed cookies, flour, cinnamon, and 1 1/2 tablespoons of the sugar. Roll the crust out to a 14 inch circle and sprinkle with the cookie mixture, leaving a 1 1/2 inch border. Arrange the blueberries over the crushed cookies, then bring up the edges to form a freeform crust.

Brush the sides of the pie with the milk. Sprinkle with the remaining sugar and bake for 30 minutes or until the sides are crisp and brown.

Warm the preserves in a saucepan over low heat and brush over the berries. Cool to room temperature, then dust the crust with sifted confectioners' sugar.

Serves 6–8

Rhubarb pie

Crust
2 cups all-purpose flour
2 tablespoons unsalted butter, chilled
    and cubed
¼ cup vegetable shortening
2 tablespoons confectioners' sugar
⅔ cup ice water

3 lb. 5 oz. rhubarb, trimmed and cut
    into ¾ inch pieces
1 cup superfine sugar
½ teaspoon ground cinnamon
2½ tablespoons cornstarch, mixed
    with ¼ cup water
2 tablespoons unsalted butter, cubed
1 egg, lightly beaten
confectioners' sugar, to dust

Grease a 10 x 8 x 1½ inch ceramic pie dish. Sift the flour and ½ teaspoon salt into a bowl and rub in the butter and shortening until the mixture looks like bread crumbs. Stir in the confectioners' sugar. Make a well, add most of the water, and mix with a flat-bladed knife, using a cutting action, until it comes together in beads. Add more water if needed. Gather the dough together and put on a floured surface. Press into a ball, flatten a little, and cover in plastic wrap. Refrigerate for 30 minutes.

Put the rhubarb, sugar, cinnamon, and 2 tablespoons water in a saucepan and stir over low heat until the sugar dissolves. Simmer, covered, for 5–8 minutes or until the rhubarb is tender. Add the cornstarch and water mixture. Bring to a boil, stirring until thickened. Cool. Preheat the oven to 350°F and heat a cookie sheet.

Roll out two-thirds of the dough to a 12 inch circle and put into the pie dish. Spoon in the rhubarb and dot with butter. Roll out the remaining crust for a lid. Brush the pie rim with egg and press the top in place. Trim the edges and make a slit in the top. Decorate with crust scraps and brush with egg. Bake on the hot cookie sheet for 35 minutes or until golden. Dust with confectioners' sugar.

Serves 6

Mixed berry tartlets

Crust
2³/₄ cups all-purpose flour
small pinch of salt
²/₃ cup unsalted butter
³/₄ cup confectioners' sugar
2 eggs, beaten

Frangipane
1 cup unsalted butter, softened
2 cups confectioners' sugar
2¹/₂ cups ground almonds
¹/₃ cup all-purpose flour
5 eggs, lightly beaten

1³/₄ cups mixed berries
  (blueberries, raspberries,
  strawberries, blackberries)
3 tablespoons apricot preserves

To make the crust, sift the flour and salt onto a work surface and make a well in the center. Put the butter into the well and mix, using a pecking action with your fingertips and thumb, until it is very soft. Add the sugar to the butter and mix. Add the eggs to the butter and mix together.

Gradually add the flour, flicking it onto the mixture, then chop through until a rough dough forms. Bring together and knead a few times until smooth. Roll into a ball, cover in plastic wrap, and refrigerate for 1 hour.

To make the frangipane, beat the butter until soft. Add the confectioners' sugar, almonds, and flour and beat well. Add the beaten eggs gradually, beating well. Put in a clean bowl, cover with plastic wrap, and refrigerate for up to 24 hours.

Preheat the oven to 350°F. Roll out the crust to ³/₄ inch thick and use to line ten 3 inch tartlet pans. Put the frangipane in a pastry bag and pipe into the pans. Put the pans on a cookie sheet and bake for 10 minutes or until golden. Cool slightly on a wire rack, then arrange the berries on top. Melt the preserves with 1 teaspoon water, strain to remove any lumps, and brush over the berries.

Makes 10

Mango and passion fruit tarts

1½ lb. store-bought or homemade
  piecrust (see page 391)
3 ripe mangoes, peeled and sliced or
  chopped, or 13 oz. can mango
  slices, drained
¼ cup passion fruit pulp, strained
1 tablespoon custard powder
⅓ cup superfine sugar
1 egg, lightly beaten
confectioners' sugar, to dust

Preheat the oven to 375°F. Grease six 4 inch (top) x 3 inch (bottom) x 1¼ inch (deep) fluted tart pans or round pie dishes. Roll out two-thirds of the crust between two sheets of waxed paper to a thickness of ⅛ inch. Cut out six 5 inch circles. Line the pans with the circles and trim the edges. Refrigerate while you make the filling.

Combine the mango, passion fruit, custard powder, and sugar in a bowl.

Roll out the remaining crust between two sheets of waxed paper to ⅛ inch thick. Cut out six 4½ inch circles. Roll out the remaining crust trimmings and cut into shapes for decoration.

Fill the crust cases with the mango mixture and brush the edges with egg. Top with the crust circles and press the edges to seal. Trim the edges and decorate with the crust shapes. Brush the tops with beaten egg and dust with confectioners' sugar.

Bake for 20–25 minutes or until the crust is golden brown. Delicious served with whipped cream.

Makes 6

Banana cream pie

13 oz. store-bought or homemade
 sweet piecrust (see page 390)
½ cup semisweet chocolate chips
4 egg yolks
½ cup superfine sugar
½ teaspoon vanilla extract
2 tablespoons custard powder
2 cups milk
2 tablespoons unsalted butter,
 softened
1 teaspoon brandy or rum
3 large ripe bananas, cut into
 1¼ inch slices
sliced banana, extra, to decorate
1¾ oz. semisweet chocolate, grated
 or shaved, to decorate

Roll out the crust between two sheets of waxed paper to line the bottom of a 9 inch (top) x 7 inch (bottom) x 1¼ inch (deep) pie pan. Remove the top sheet of paper and invert the pastry into the pan (see page 392). Trim the excess. Refrigerate for 20 minutes.

Preheat the oven to 375°F. Line the crust with crumpled waxed paper and cover with baking beads or rice. Bake for 10 minutes, remove the paper and beads, then bake for 10 minutes or until the crust is dry and cooked through. While still hot, cover with chocolate chips. Leave for 5 minutes, then spread the melted chocolate over the bottom.

Put the egg yolks, sugar, vanilla, and custard powder in a bowl and beat with an electric mixer for 2–3 minutes or until thick. Bring the milk to a boil in a saucepan over medium heat, remove from the heat, and gradually pour into the egg mixture, stirring well. Return the custard filling to the saucepan and bring to a boil, stirring well. Cook for 2 minutes or until thick. Remove from the heat, stir in the butter and brandy, and allow to cool. Arrange the banana slices over the chocolate, then pour the custard on top. Decorate with extra banana slices and the grated chocolate.

Serves 6–8

Nutty fig pie

13 oz. store-bought or homemade
  sweet piecrust (see page 390)
1 1/2 cups hazelnuts
2/3 cup pine nuts
1 cup sliced almonds
2/3 cup blanched almonds
2/3 cup whipping cream
1/4 cup unsalted butter
1/4 cup honey
. 1/2 cup light brown sugar
5 oz. dessert figs, cut into quarters
chocolate ice cream, to serve

Preheat the oven to 400°F and grease a 9 inch (top) x 7 inch (bottom) x 1 1/4 inch (deep) pie pan. Roll the crust out between two sheets of waxed paper until large enough to cover the bottom and side of the pie pan. Remove the top sheet and invert the crust into the pan, allowing any excess to hang over. Trim with a knife and prick the bottom several times with a fork. Score the edge with a fork. Refrigerate for 20 minutes, then bake for 15 minutes or until crisp, dry, and pale golden. Allow to cool.

Bake the hazelnuts on a cookie sheet for 8 minutes or until the skins start to peel away. Transfer to a dish towel and rub to remove the skins. Place the pine nuts, sliced almonds, and blanched almonds on a cookie sheet and bake for 5–6 minutes or until pale golden.

Place the cream, butter, honey, and brown sugar in a saucepan and stir over medium heat until the sugar dissolves and the butter melts. Remove from the heat and stir in the nuts and figs. Spoon the mixture into the crust case and bake for 30 minutes. Remove and cool until firm before slicing. Delicious served with chocolate ice cream.

Serves 8

Apricot and almond tart

13 oz. store-bought or homemade
piecrust (see page 391)
1 1/4 cups dried apricots
1/3 cup brandy or grappa
confectioners' sugar, to dust
crème fraîche or whipped cream,
to serve

Almond filling
3/4 cup unsalted butter, softened
3/4 cup superfine sugar
2 cups sliced blanched almonds
2 eggs
1 teaspoon vanilla extract
1 heaping teaspoon all-purpose flour

Grease a 10 inch, loose-bottomed metal tart pan. Dust the work surface with flour and roll out the crust to fit the pan. Line the pan and trim the edges. Refrigerate for 15 minutes. Preheat the oven to 400°F.

Line the crust shell with crumpled waxed paper and baking beads and bake for 12 minutes, then remove the paper and beads—if the crust still looks wet, dry it out in the oven for 5 minutes. Cool for a few minutes. Reduce the oven to 350°F.

Put the dried apricots and brandy in a saucepan and cook over low heat for about 5 minutes or until most of the liquid has evaporated. Allow to cool.

To make the almond filling, use a food processor to cream the butter and sugar until light and pale. Add the almonds, eggs, vanilla, and flour and briefly blend. (If you overbeat it, the mixture may separate.) Spoon the filling into the crust shell, then place the apricots in the shell, arranging them in two circles, one inside the other. Bake for 30–40 minutes or until the filling is set. Cool and sprinkle with confectioners' sugar just before serving. Serve with crème fraîche or whipped cream.

Serves 8

Blackberry pie

1 lb. store-bought or homemade
  piecrust (see page 391)
4 cups blackberries
$2/3$ cup superfine sugar
2 tablespoons cornstarch
milk, to brush
1 egg, lightly beaten
superfine sugar, extra, to sprinkle

Preheat the oven to 400°F. Grease a 10 inch (top) x 8^3/$_4$ inch (bottom) x 1^3/$_4$ inch (deep) ceramic pie dish. Roll out two-thirds of the crust between two sheets of waxed paper until large enough to line the bottom and side of the pie dish. Remove the top paper, invert the crust into the dish, and press firmly into place, allowing the excess to hang over the edges.

Toss the blackberries (if frozen, thaw and drain well), sugar, and cornstarch together in a bowl until well mixed, then transfer to the pie dish. Roll out the remaining crust between two sheets of waxed paper until large enough to cover the pie. Moisten the rim of the pie base with milk and press the crust lid firmly into place. Trim and crimp the edges. Brush with egg and sprinkle with the extra sugar. Pierce the top of the pie with a knife.

Bake on the bottom shelf of the oven for 10 minutes. Reduce the oven to 350°F and move the pie to the center shelf. Bake for another 30 minutes or until golden on top. Cool before serving with whipped cream or ice cream.

Serves 6

Portuguese custard tarts

1 1/4 cups all-purpose flour
1 tablespoon vegetable shortening,
  chopped and softened
2 tablespoons unsalted butter,
  chopped and softened
1 cup sugar
2 cups milk
3 tablespoons cornstarch
1 tablespoon custard powder
4 egg yolks
1 teaspoon vanilla extract

Sift the flour into a bowl. Add 3/4 cup water, or enough to form a soft dough. Gather into a ball, then roll out on waxed paper to form a 10 x 12 inch rectangle. Spread the shortening over the surface. Roll up from the short edge to form a log.

Roll the dough out into a rectangle again and spread with the butter. Roll into a log and slice into twelve pieces. Working out from the center, use your fingertips to press each round out to a circle large enough to cover the bottom and sides of twelve 1/3 cup muffin cups. Press into the pan and refrigerate.

Put the sugar and 1/3 cup water into a saucepan and stir over low heat until the sugar dissolves. Mix a little milk with the cornstarch and custard powder to form a smooth paste and add to the saucepan with the remaining milk, egg yolks, and vanilla. Stir over low heat until thickened. Put in a bowl, cover, and cool.

Preheat the oven to 425°F. Divide the filling among the crust bases. Bake for 30 minutes or until the custard is set and the tops have browned. Cool in the pans, then transfer to a wire rack.

Makes 12

Pear and almond flan

1¼ cups all-purpose flour
⅓ cup unsalted butter, chilled
  and chopped
¼ cup superfine sugar
2 egg yolks

Filling
⅔ cup unsalted butter, softened
⅔ cup superfine sugar
3 eggs
2¼ cups ground almonds
1½ tablespoons all-purpose flour
2 ripe pears, peeled, halved
  lengthwise, cores removed

Grease a shallow, 10 inch round tart pan with a removable base. Put the flour, butter, and superfine sugar in a food processor and process until the mixture resembles bread crumbs. Add the egg yolks and about 1 tablespoon of water until the mixture just comes together. Turn out onto a floured surface and gather into a ball. Cover in plastic wrap and refrigerate for 30 minutes. Preheat the oven to 350°F.

Roll the crust between waxed paper dusted with flour and line the pan with the crust. Trim off any excess. Prick the base a few times. Blind bake the crust for 10 minutes (see page 392). Remove the paper and beads and bake for another 10 minutes.

To make the filling, mix the butter and sugar with an electric mixer for 30 seconds only. Add the eggs one at a time, beating after each addition. Fold in the ground almonds and flour and spread the filling over the cooled base. Cut the pears crosswise into 1¼ inch slices, separate them slightly, then place on top of the tart to form a cross. Bake for 50 minutes or until the filling has set (the middle may still be a little soft). Cool in the pan, then refrigerate for 2 hours before serving.

Serves 8

Lemon meringue pie

13 oz. store-bought or homemade
  sweet piecrust (see page 391)
$1/4$ cup all-purpose flour
$1/4$ cup cornstarch
1 cup superfine sugar
$3/4$ cup lemon juice
1 tablespoon grated lemon zest
$1/4$ cup unsalted butter, chopped
6 egg yolks
1 quantity meringue (see page 393)

Grease a 10 inch (top) x 7 inch (bottom) x 1$1/4$ inch (deep) pie plate. Roll the crust out between two sheets of waxed paper into a 12 inch circle. Invert the crust into the pie plate. Trim the edges. Reroll the crust trimmings and cut into three 4 x $3/4$ inch strips. Brush the pie rim with water, place the crust strips around the top, and use your fingers to make a decorative edge. Prick over the base with a fork. Cover and refrigerate for 20 minutes. Preheat the oven to 350°F.

Blind bake the crust for 15 minutes (see page 392). Remove the beads and bake for 15–20 minutes. Cool.

Increase the oven to 400°F. Put the flours, sugar, lemon juice, and zest in a saucepan. Gradually add 1$1/4$ cups water and whisk over medium heat until smooth. Cook, stirring, for 2 minutes or until thick. Remove from the heat and vigorously whisk in the butter and egg yolks. Return to low heat and stir constantly for 2 minutes or until very thick.

Spread the lemon filling into the crust base, then cover with the meringue, piling high in the center and making peaks with a knife. Bake for 8–10 minutes or until lightly browned.

Serves 4–6

Old-fashioned apple pie

Crust
2 cups self-rising flour
²/₃ cup cornstarch
³/₄ cup unsalted butter, chilled
  and cubed
¹/₃ cup superfine sugar
1 egg, lightly beaten

2 tablespoons unsalted butter
6 green apples, peeled, cored,
  and thinly sliced
1 tablespoon lemon juice
³/₄ cup light brown sugar
1 teaspoon ground nutmeg
2 tablespoons all-purpose flour
  mixed with ¹/₄ cup water
¹/₄ cup ground almonds
milk, to brush
sugar, to sprinkle

Lightly grease an 8 inch metal pie dish. Sift the flours into a large bowl and rub in the butter with your fingers until the mixture resembles fine bread crumbs. Stir in the sugar and a pinch of salt. Make a well, add the egg, and mix with a knife, using a cutting action, until the mixture comes together in beads. Put the dough on a floured surface and press into a smooth disk, cover with plastic wrap, and refrigerate for 20 minutes.

Use two-thirds of the dough to line the bottom and side of the dish (see page 392). Roll out the remaining dough to make a lid. Cover and refrigerate for 20 minutes. Preheat the oven to 400°F and heat a cookie sheet.

Melt the butter in a large frying pan, add the apple slices, and toss. Stir in the lemon juice, sugar, and nutmeg and cook for 10 minutes or until tender. Add the flour and water mixture, then the almonds. Bring to a boil and cook, stirring, for 2–3 minutes. Pour into a bowl and cool. Put the apples in the crust case. Cover with the crust lid and press lightly onto the rim. Trim the edges and pinch together to seal. Prick over the top, brush with milk, and sprinkle with sugar. Bake on the hot cookie sheet for 40 minutes or until golden.

Serves 8

Almond pies

½ cup sliced almonds
½ cup unsalted butter, softened
1 cup confectioners' sugar
1¼ cups ground almonds
¼ cup all-purpose flour
2 eggs
1 tablespoon rum or brandy
1 teaspoon almond extract
½ teaspoon vanilla extract
4 sheets store-bought frozen puff
   pastry, thawed
1 egg, lightly beaten
sugar, to sprinkle
confectioners' sugar, to dust

Preheat the oven to 400°F. Bake the sliced almonds on a cookie sheet for 2–3 minutes or until just golden. Remove and return the cookie sheet to the oven to keep it hot.

Beat together the butter, confectioners' sugar, ground almonds, flour, eggs, rum, almond extract, and vanilla with an electric mixer for 2–3 minutes or until smooth and combined. Fold in the sliced almonds.

Cut out eight 4 inch rounds and eight 4½ inch rounds from the puff pastry. Spread the smaller rounds with equal amounts of filling, leaving a ½ inch border. Brush the borders with beaten egg and cover with the tops. Seal the edges with a fork and, if you wish, decorate the tops with shapes cut from pastry scraps.

Pierce with a fork to allow steam to escape. Brush with egg and sprinkle with sugar. Bake on the hot cookie sheet for 15–20 minutes or until the pastry is puffed and golden. Dust with confectioners' sugar before serving.

Makes 8

Peach pie

1 lb. store-bought or homemade
   sweet piecrust (see page 391)
2 x 1 lb. 14 oz. cans peach slices,
   well-drained
½ cup superfine sugar
¼ cup cornstarch
¼ teaspoon almond extract
1 tablespoon unsalted butter,
   chopped
1 tablespoon milk
1 egg, lightly beaten
superfine sugar, to sprinkle

Roll out two-thirds of the dough between two sheets of waxed paper until large enough to line a 9 inch (top) x 7 inch (bottom) x 1¼ inch (deep) pie pan. Remove the top sheet of paper and invert the crust into the pan. Use a small ball of dough to press the crust into the pan. Trim any excess crust with a knife. Refrigerate for 20 minutes.

Preheat the oven to 400°F. Line the crust with crumpled waxed paper and pour in baking beads or rice. Bake for 10 minutes, remove the paper and beads, and return to the oven for 5 minutes or until the crust base is dry and pale golden. Allow to cool.

Mix the peaches, sugar, cornstarch, and almond extract in a bowl, then spoon into the crust. Dot with butter and moisten the edges with milk.

Roll out the remaining dough to a 10 inch square. Using a fluted pastry cutter, cut into ten strips 1 inch wide. Lay the strips in a lattice pattern over the filling, pressing firmly on the edges, and trim. Brush with egg and sprinkle with sugar. Bake for 10 minutes, reduce the heat to 350°F, and bake for 30 minutes or until golden. Cool before serving.

Serves 6

Berry ricotta cream tartlets

Crust
1 1/2 cups all-purpose flour
1 cup ground almonds
1/3 cup confectioners' sugar
1/2 cup unsalted butter, chopped
1 egg, lightly beaten

Filling
3/4 cup ricotta cheese
1 teaspoon vanilla extract
2 eggs
2/3 cup superfine sugar
1/2 cup whipping cream
1/2 cup raspberries
1/2 cup blueberries
confectioners' sugar, to dust

Sift the flour into a bowl, then add the almonds and confectioners' sugar. Cut the butter into the flour with a pastry blender or rub in with your fingertips until it resembles bread crumbs. Make a well in the center, add the egg, and mix with a flat-bladed knife, using a cutting action, until the mixture comes together in beads. Gather the dough and put onto a lightly floured surface. Press into a ball, cover with plastic wrap, and refrigerate for 30 minutes.

Grease six 3 inch (1 1/4 inch deep), loose-bottomed tart pans. Divide the crust into six and roll each piece out between two sheets of waxed paper to fit the bottom and side of the pans. Press the crust into the pans, trim the edges, and prick the bases with a fork. Refrigerate for 30 minutes. Preheat the oven to 350°F. Line the crust with crumpled waxed paper and spread with baking beads or rice. Bake for 8–10 minutes, then remove the paper and beads.

Process the ricotta, vanilla, eggs, sugar, and cream in a food processor until smooth. Divide the berries and filling among the tarts and bake for 25–30 minutes or until the filling is just set—the top should be soft but not too wobbly. Cool. Dust with confectioners' sugar and serve.

Serves 6

Pear and apple crumble pie

13 oz. store-bought or homemade
   piecrust (see page 390)
3 pears, peeled, cored, and sliced
4 Granny Smith apples, peeled,
   cored, and sliced
1/4 cup superfine sugar
2 teaspoons grated orange zest
3/4 cup raisins
3/4 cup all-purpose flour
1/2 cup light brown sugar
1/2 teaspoon ground ginger
1/3 cup unsalted butter
whipped cream, to serve

Roll the crust between two sheets
of waxed paper until large enough to
cover the bottom and side of a 9 inch
(top) x 7 inch (bottom) x 1 1/4 inch
(deep) pie dish. Remove the top sheet
of waxed paper and invert the crust
into the dish. Trim the excess. Cover
with plastic wrap and refrigerate for
20 minutes.

Put the sliced fruit in a large
saucepan. Add the sugar, zest, and
2 tablespoons water and cook over
low heat, stirring occasionally for
20 minutes or until the fruit is tender
but still holding its shape. Remove
from the heat, add the raisins and a
pinch of salt, and mix. Cool, then
spoon into the crust case.

Preheat the oven to 400°F and
preheat a cookie sheet. To make the
topping, combine the flour, brown
sugar, and ginger in a bowl and rub
in the butter with your fingertips until
the mixture resembles coarse bread
crumbs. Sprinkle over the fruit.

Place the pie dish on the hot cookie
sheet, bake for 10 minutes, then
reduce the oven temperature to 350°F
and cook the pie for 40 minutes or
until nicely browned. Cover the pie
with aluminum foil halfway through if
the top is browning too quickly. Serve
warm with whipped cream.

Serves 6–8

Key lime pie

13 oz. store-bought or homemade
   sweet piecrust (see page 391)
4 egg yolks
14 oz. can condensed milk
½ cup lime juice
2 teaspoons grated lime zest
lime slices, to garnish
confectioners' sugar, to dust
whipped cream, to serve

Preheat the oven to 350°F. Grease a 9 inch, loose-bottomed tart pan. Roll the dough out between two sheets of waxed paper until it is large enough to fit into the tart pan. Remove the top sheet of paper and invert the crust into the pan. Use a small ball of dough to help press the crust into the pan, allowing any excess to hang over the sides. Use a small, sharp knife to trim away any extra crust.

Line the crust shell with a piece of crumpled waxed paper that is large enough to cover the bottom and side of the pan and pour in some baking beads or rice. Bake for 10 minutes, remove the paper and beads, and return the crust to the oven for another 4–5 minutes or until the base is dry. Allow to cool.

Using an electric mixer, beat the egg yolks, condensed milk, lime juice, and zest in a large bowl for 2 minutes or until well combined. Pour into the pie shell and smooth the surface. Bake for 20–25 minutes or until set. Allow the pie to cool, then refrigerate for 2 hours or until well chilled. Garnish with lime slices, dust with sifted confectioners' sugar, and serve with whipped cream.

Serves 6–8

Honey and pine nut tart

Crust
2 cups all-purpose flour
1½ tablespoons confectioners' sugar
½ cup unsalted butter, chilled and
  chopped
1 egg, lightly beaten

Filling
½ cup honey
½ cup unsalted butter, softened
½ cup superfine sugar
3 eggs, lightly beaten
¼ teaspoon vanilla extract
1 tablespoon almond liqueur
1 teaspoon finely grated lemon zest
1 tablespoon lemon juice
1½ cups pine nuts, toasted
  (see page 390)
confectioners' sugar, to dust
crème fraîche or mascarpone,
  to serve

Preheat the oven to 375°F and place
a cookie sheet on the middle shelf.
Grease a 9 inch, loose-bottomed
tart pan.

Roll out the crust between two sheets
of waxed paper to a ⅛ inch thick
circle. Invert the crust into the pan,
pressing it into the side and base of
the pan. Trim any excess. Prick all
over the base and chill for 15 minutes.
Cut out three leaves about 1½ inches
long from the crust scraps. Cover
and chill. Line the crust with waxed
paper and fill with baking beads. Bake
on the cookie sheet for 10 minutes,
then remove.

Reduce the oven to 350°F. To make
the filling, heat the honey in a
saucepan until runny. Beat the butter
and sugar in a bowl until smooth and
pale. Gradually add the eggs, beating
after each addition. Mix in the honey,
vanilla, liqueur, lemon zest and juice,
and a pinch of salt. Stir in the toasted
pine nuts, spoon into the crust, and
smooth over. Arrange the crust leaves
in the center.

Bake on the hot cookie sheet for
40 minutes or until set. Cover the top
with aluminum foil after 25 minutes.
Serve warm, dusted with
confectioners' sugar. Serve with
crème fraîche or mascarpone.

Serves 6

Raisin pie

1 ¼ lb. store-bought or homemade
  sweet piecrust (see page 391)
⅓ cup orange juice
2 tablespoons lemon juice
2 ½ cups raisins
¾ cup light brown sugar
½ teaspoon pumpkin pie spice
¼ cup cornstarch
1 teaspoon finely grated lemon zest
1 teaspoon finely grated orange zest
1 egg, lightly beaten
1 tablespoon sugar, to sprinkle

Preheat the oven to 375°F and heat a cookie sheet. Grease a 9 inch (top) x 7 inch (base) x 1 ¼ inch (deep) pie pan. Roll out two-thirds of the crust between two sheets of waxed paper to fit the bottom and side of the dish. Remove the top paper and invert the crust into the pan, pressing it into the pan. Trim the excess. Chill the base and remaining crust.

Combine the citrus juices, raisins, and 1 cup water in a saucepan. Boil over high heat, stirring occasionally, for 2 minutes. Remove from the heat.

Mix the brown sugar, pumpkin pie spice, and cornstarch in a bowl. Add ½ cup water and mix until smooth. Slowly stir into the raisin mixture and return the saucepan to the stove over high heat. Boil, stirring, then reduce to a simmer, stirring occasionally, for 5 minutes or until it thickens. Stir in the citrus zest and cool for 30 minutes.

Roll out the remaining crust to cover the pie. Fill the base with the raisin mixture, brush the edges with the egg, and cover with the crust top. Pinch the edges together and make a few small holes. Brush with egg, sprinkle with sugar, and bake on the cookie sheet for 40 minutes or until golden. Serve warm or cold.

Serves 6–8

Lime and blueberry pie

13 oz. store-bought or homemade
  sweet piecrust (see page 391)
3 eggs
1/2 cup superfine sugar
1/4 cup buttermilk
1 tablespoon lime juice
2 teaspoons grated lime zest
2 tablespoons custard powder
1 2/3 cups blueberries
confectioners' sugar, to dust

Roll out the crust between two sheets of waxed paper to line a 9 inch (top) x 7 inch (base) x 1 1/4 inch (deep) pie pan. Remove the top paper and invert the crust into the pan. Use a small ball of dough to press the crust into the pan. Trim any excess crust. Refrigerate for 20 minutes.

Preheat the oven to 400°F. Line the base and side of the crust with crumpled waxed paper and pour in baking beads or rice. Bake for 10 minutes, remove the paper and beads, and bake for 4–5 minutes or until the base is dry and lightly colored. Cool slightly. Reduce the oven to 350°F.

To make the filling, beat the eggs and superfine sugar in a bowl with an electric mixer until the mixture is thick and pale. Add the buttermilk, lime juice, zest, and sifted custard powder. Stir until combined, then spoon into the crust shell. Bake for 15 minutes, then reduce the temperature to 315°F and bake for another 20–25 minutes or until the filling has colored slightly and is set. Cool (the filling will sink while cooling), then top with the blueberries. Dust with sifted confectioners' sugar and serve.

Serves 6–8

Apple galette

1 sheet frozen puff pastry, thawed
¼ cup apricot preserves
1 Granny Smith apple
2 teaspoons raw sugar

Preheat the oven to 415°F. Place a cookie sheet in the oven to heat. Trim the corners from the pastry to make a neat circle (use a large plate as a guide if you like).

Place the apricot preserves in a small saucepan and stir over low heat to warm through and thin. Pass through a strainer to remove any pieces of fruit, then brush over the puff pastry, leaving a ½ inch border.

Peel, halve, and core the apple, then cut into ⅛ inch thick slices. Arrange over the pastry in an overlapping circular pattern, leaving a ½ inch border around the edge. Sprinkle evenly with the sugar.

Carefully place the galette on a lightly greased cookie sheet and bake for 35 minutes or until the edge of the pastry is well browned and puffed.

Serves 6

Butternut squash pie

Crust

1¼ cups all-purpose flour
½ cup unsalted butter, chilled
   and cubed
2 teaspoons superfine sugar
4 tablespoons ice water

1½ lb. butternut squash, cubed,
   boiled, and mashed, then pushed
   through a strainer and cooled
2 eggs, lightly beaten
1 cup light brown sugar
⅓ cup whipping cream
1 tablespoon sweet sherry or brandy
½ teaspoon ground ginger
½ teaspoon ground nutmeg
1 teaspoon ground cinnamon

Sift the flour into a bowl and cut in the butter with a pastry blender or rub in with your fingertips until the mixture resembles bread crumbs. Mix in the superfine sugar. Make a well in the center, add almost all the water, and mix with a flat-bladed knife, using a cutting action, until the mixture comes together in beads—add more water if needed. Gather the dough and put on a lightly floured surface. Press into a ball and flatten slightly. Cover in plastic wrap. Refrigerate for 20 minutes.

Roll out the crust between two sheets of waxed paper large enough to cover the bottom and side of a 9 inch (top) x 7 inch (bottom) x 1¼ inch (deep) pie dish. Line the dish with crust, trim the excess, and crimp the edges with a fork. Cover with plastic wrap and refrigerate for 20 minutes. Preheat the oven to 350°F. Line the crust shell with crumpled waxed paper. Pour in baking beads and bake for 10 minutes, then remove the paper and beads. Bake for 10 minutes or until pale golden. Allow to cool.

Whisk the eggs and sugar in a bowl. Stir in the cooled squash, cream, sherry, and the spices. Pour into the crust shell and bake for 1 hour or until set—cover the edges with aluminum foil if overbrowning. Cool before serving.

Serves 6–8

Apple tarte tatin

1/3 cup unsalted butter, chopped
3/4 cup sugar
6 large pink lady, fuji, or golden
   delicious apples, peeled, cored,
   and quartered
1 sheet store-bought puff pastry
whipped cream or ice cream,
   to serve

Preheat the oven to 425°F. Lightly grease a shallow, 9 inch cake pan. Melt the unsalted butter in a frying pan, add the sugar, and cook, stirring, over medium heat for 4–5 minutes or until the sugar starts to caramelize and turn brown. Continue to cook, stirring, until the caramel turns golden brown.

Add the apples to the pan and cook over low heat for 20–25 minutes or until they start to turn golden brown. Carefully turn the apples over and cook the other side until evenly colored. Cook off any liquid from the apples over a higher heat—the caramel should be sticky rather than runny. Remove from the heat. Using tongs, arrange the hot apples in circles in the cake pan and pour the sauce on top.

Place the pastry over the apples to cover, tucking the pastry down firmly at the edges using the end of a spoon. Bake for 30–35 minutes or until the pastry is cooked. Allow the tarte tatin to cool for 15 minutes before inverting onto a serving plate. Remove the paper and serve warm or cold with whipped cream or ice cream.

Serves 6

Tarte au citron

Crust
2³/₄ cups all-purpose flour
small pinch of salt
²/₃ cup unsalted butter
³/₄ cup confectioners' sugar
2 eggs, beaten

Filling
4 eggs
2 egg yolks
1¹/₄ cups superfine sugar
³/₄ cup heavy cream
1 cup lemon juice
finely grated zest of 3 lemons

To make the crust, sift the flour and salt onto a work surface and make a well. Put the butter into the well and work, using a pecking action with your fingertips and thumb, until it is very soft. Add the sugar to the butter and mix. Add the eggs to the butter and mix. Gradually incorporate the flour, flicking it onto the mixture, then chop through it until you have a rough dough. Bring together, knead a few times to make a smooth dough, then roll into a ball. Cover in plastic wrap and refrigerate for at least 1 hour.

Preheat the oven to 375°F. Roll out the crust to line a 9 inch, loose-bottomed, fluted tart pan. Chill for 20 minutes. To make the filling, whisk together the eggs, egg yolks, and sugar. Add the cream, whisking all the time, then mix in the lemon juice and zest.

Blind bake the crust (see page 392) for 10 minutes, remove the paper, and bake for 3–5 minutes or until the crust is just cooked. Remove from the oven and reduce the oven to 300°F. Put the tart pan on a cookie sheet and carefully pour the filling into the crust case. Return to the oven for 35–40 minutes or until set. Cool before serving.

Serves 8

Chocolate fudge pecan pie

Crust
1 1/4 cups all-purpose flour
2 tablespoons cocoa powder
2 tablespoons light brown sugar
1/3 cup unsalted butter, chilled
  and cubed
2–3 tablespoons ice water

Filling
2 cups pecans, roughly chopped
3 1/2 oz. semisweet chocolate,
  chopped
1/2 cup light brown sugar
2/3 cup light or dark corn syrup
3 eggs, lightly beaten
2 teaspoons vanilla extract

Grease a 9 inch (top) x 7 inch (bottom) x 1 1/4 inch (deep) pie dish. Sift the flour, cocoa, and sugar into a bowl and cut in the butter with a pastry blender or rub in with your fingertips until the mixture resembles fine bread crumbs. Make a well, add almost all the water, and mix with a knife, adding more water if necessary.

Gather the dough together and lift onto a sheet of waxed paper. Press the dough into a circle and refrigerate for 20 minutes. Roll out the crust between two sheets of waxed paper to fit the dish. Line the dish and trim the edges. Refrigerate for 20 minutes.

Preheat the oven to 350°F. Cover the crust with crumpled waxed paper and fill with baking beads or rice. Bake for 15 minutes, then remove the paper and beads and bake for 15–20 minutes or until the base is dry. Cool completely.

Place the pie dish on a cookie sheet to catch any drips. Spread the pecans and chocolate over the crust. Combine the sugar, corn syrup, eggs, and vanilla in a bowl and whisk together with a fork. Pour into the crust and bake for 45 minutes (the filling will still be a bit wobbly, but will set on cooling). Allow to cool before cutting to serve.

Serves 6

Cherry pie

1 lb. store-bought or homemade
 sweet piecrust (see page 391)
1 lb. 12 oz. can seedless black
 cherries, well drained
⅓ cup light brown sugar
1½ teaspoons ground cinnamon
1 teaspoon finely grated lemon zest
1 teaspoon finely grated orange zest
1–2 drops almond extract
¼ cup ground almonds
1 egg, lightly beaten

Preheat the oven to 375°F. Roll out two-thirds of the dough between two sheets of waxed paper to form a circle large enough to fit an 8¾ inch (top) x 8 inch (bottom) x ¾ inch (deep) pie plate. Remove the top sheet of waxed paper and invert the crust into the pie plate. Cut away the excess crust with a small, sharp knife. Roll out the remaining crust large enough to cover the pie. Refrigerate, covered in plastic wrap, for 20 minutes.

Place the cherries, sugar, cinnamon, lemon and orange zests, and almond extract in a bowl and mix to coat the cherries.

Line the crust base with the ground almonds. Spoon in the filling, brush the crust edges with beaten egg, and cover with the crust lid. Use a fork to seal the crust edges. Cut four slits in the top of the pie to allow steam to escape, then brush the crust with beaten egg. Bake for 1 hour or until the crust is golden and the juices are bubbling through the slits in the crust. Serve warm.

Serves 6

Walnut pie with caramel sauce

Crust
2 cups all-purpose flour
³/₄ cup unsalted butter, chilled and
  cubed
¹/₃ cup confectioners' sugar
1 egg yolk
3–4 tablespoons ice water

Filling
2 eggs
1 cup superfine sugar
1¹/₂ cups walnuts, finely chopped

1 egg yolk, lightly beaten
confectioners' sugar, to dust
walnuts, to garnish
1 quantity caramel sauce (see
  page 393)

Sift the flour and ¹/₂ teaspoon salt into a large bowl and rub in the butter with your fingertips until the mixture resembles bread crumbs. Mix in the confectioners' sugar. Make a well, add the egg yolk and almost all the water, and mix with a flat-bladed knife, using a cutting action, until the mixture comes together in beads. Lift out onto a floured surface. Press into a ball and flatten slightly. Cover in plastic wrap. Refrigerate for 20 minutes.

Preheat the oven to 350°F. Grease a fluted, 14 inch pie pan. Place the eggs and sugar in a bowl and beat with a spoon or whisk for 2 minutes. Stir in the walnuts.

Divide the dough into two portions, one slightly larger than the other. Line the bottom and side of the pan with the larger portion (see page 392). Cover in plastic wrap and refrigerate. Roll out the remaining crust for a lid.

Pour the walnut filling into the shell, brush the rim with egg yolk, and cover with the lid, pressing the edges to seal. Trim the edge. Make a slit in the top. Brush with egg yolk and bake for 30–35 minutes. Cool at room temperature for at least 1 hour. Dust with confectioners' sugar and sprinkle with walnuts. Drizzle with caramel sauce.

Serves 6–8

Basics

Toasting nuts

Toasting nuts before use enhances their flavor.

Spread the nuts on a cookie sheet and toast in a 350°F oven for 5–8 minutes or until they are lightly colored. Once they start to brown, nuts burn very quickly, so watch them carefully.

Melting chocolate

When melting chocolate, always use a clean, dry bowl. Water or moisture will make the chocolate seize (i.e., turn into a thick mass that won't melt), and overheating will make it scorch and taste bitter.

To melt chocolate, chop it into small, evenly sized pieces and place in a heatproof bowl. Bring a saucepan of water to a boil, then remove from the heat. Position the bowl over the saucepan of water—make sure the bowl doesn't touch the water and that no water or steam gets into the bowl or the chocolate will seize. Allow the chocolate to soften a little, then stir until smooth and melted.

Remove the chocolate from the saucepan to cool, or leave in place over the hot water if you want to keep the chocolate liquid.

Piecrust

This recipe makes about 12 oz. of piecrust, which is enough to line the bottom or top of a 9 inch pie dish.

To make 12 oz. of piecrust, you will need 2 cups all-purpose flour, ½ cup chilled butter chopped into small pieces, and 2–3 tablespoons ice water. To line the top and base, you will need 1¼ lb. of crust. For this you need 3¼ cups all-purpose flour, ¾ cup chilled butter chopped into small pieces, and 3–4 tablespoons ice water.

Sift the flour and ¼ teaspoon salt into a large bowl. Sifting the flour aerates the dough and helps make the finished crust crisp and light.

Add the chopped butter and cut it into the flour with a pastry blender or rub in with your fingertips (not your palms, as they tend to be too warm) until the mixture resembles fine bread crumbs. As you rub the butter into the flour, lift it up high and let it fall back into the bowl. If applicable, stir in the other dry ingredients such as sugar (if making sweet piecrust).

Make a well in the center, add nearly all the water, and mix with a flat-bladed knife, using a cutting (rather than a stirring) action. The mixture will come together in small beads of dough. If necessary, add more water, a teaspoon at a time, until the dough comes together. Test the dough by pinching a little piece between your fingers—if it doesn't hold together, it needs more water. Use just enough to hold the crust together—if it is too wet it will toughen and may shrink on baking; if too dry, it will be crumbly.

Gently gather the dough together and lift out onto a lightly floured surface. Press the dough into a ball and then flatten it slightly—don't knead or handle the dough too much.

Cover in plastic wrap and refrigerate for 20–30 minutes—this makes it easier to roll out the dough and helps prevent shrinkage during cooking.

Tart crust

This crust is often used for fruit pies, flans, and tarts because it gives a richer, crisper crust.

To transform a basic piecrust into a rich one, gradually add a beaten egg yolk to the flour with 2–3 tablespoons ice water. Mix with a flat-bladed knife, as described in the technique for piecrust on page 390.

Sweet piecrust

Follow the directions to make the piecrust and add 2 tablespoons superfine or confectioners' sugar after the butter has been cut into the flour. If preferred, you can also add egg yolks to enrich the crust (see the instructions for the tart crust).

Food processor piecrust

Piecrusts can be made quickly and successfully with a food processor. The obvious advantage is its speed, and you don't handle the crust as much, so it stays cool.

Process the flour and cold chopped butter in short bursts, using the pulse button if your machine has one, until the mixture resembles fine bread crumbs. While the processor is running, add a teaspoon of water at a time until the dough holds together. Process in short bursts again and don't overprocess or the crust will toughen and shrink while cooking. You will know you have overworked the crust if it forms a ball in the processor—it should just come together in clumps.

Gather it into a ball on a lightly floured surface, flatten it into a circle, and wrap in plastic wrap, then refrigerate for 20–30 minutes.

Lining the pan with crust

Remove the dough from the refrigerator. Roll out the dough between two sheets of waxed paper or plastic wrap, or on a lightly floured surface. Roll out from the center, rotating the dough, rather than rolling backward and forward.

If you used waxed paper to roll out the crust, remove the top sheet and carefully invert the crust over the pan, center it, and then peel away the paper. If you rolled out the crust on a floured surface, roll the crust back over the rolling pin so it is hanging, then ease it into the pan.

Once the crust is in the pan, quickly lift up the sides so they don't break over the sharp edges of the pan. Use a small ball of excess dough to help ease and press the crust shell into the side of the pan.

Allow the excess crust to hang over the side and, if using a tart pan, roll the rolling pin over the top of the pan to cut off the excess crust. If using a glass or ceramic pie dish, use a small, sharp knife to cut away the excess crust. If the pie or tart is to have a lid, leave the excess crust hanging over the edges of the dish—this can be trimmed once the lid is in place.

However gently you handle the dough, it is bound to shrink a little, so let it sit slightly above the side of the pan. If you rolled off the excess crust with a rolling pin, you may find the crust has bunched down the sides a little—press the crust with your thumbs to flatten and lift it.

Refrigerate in the pan for 15 minutes to relax the crust and prevent or minimize shrinkage.

Blind baking

If the crust is to have a moist filling, it will probably require partial blind baking to prevent the base from becoming soggy.

When blind baking, the crust needs some weights put on it to keep it from rising. Cover the base and side of the crust shell with a piece of crumpled waxed paper. Pour in some baking beads, dried beans, or uncooked rice.

Bake the crust shell for the recommended time (usually 10 minutes), then remove the paper and weights and return the crust to the oven for 10–15 minutes, or as specified in the recipe, until the base is dry with no greasy patches. Allow to cool completely.

Cooked filling should also be cooled before putting it in the crust shell in order to prevent soggy crust.

Making and testing sugar syrup

When making sugar syrup, put the sugar and water (or other liquid ingredients) into a saucepan and stir over low heat until the sugar dissolves. It is important that the sugar has dissolved completely before raising the heat. Bring to a rolling boil, boiling for the time specified in the recipe. Do not stir the liquid once it is boiling. Use a wet pastry brush to brush the side of the pan to prevent crystals from forming.

A sugar thermometer is helpful for determining the exact temperature and stages of the boiled sugar syrup. The correct temperature is very important, or the mixture will not set properly. If you don't have a thermometer, the syrup can be tested by dropping about 1/4 teaspoon of the syrup into a glass or bowl of ice water, then molding the ball between your fingers.

At soft ball (234–240°F) stage, a blob of syrup when dropped in cold water will form a very soft ball, but will lose its shape in the air.

At firm ball (245–250°F) stage, the syrup will be firmer but still pliable and will lose its shape in the air.

At hard ball (250–265°F) stage, a blob of syrup will form a very firm but pliable ball that will hold its shape at room temperature.

At soft crack (265–290°F) stage, the ball of sugar will stretch to form slightly sticky threads.

At hard crack (290–315°F) stage, the ball can be stretched to form brittle threads.

Meringue

To make one quantity of meringue, beat 6 egg whites and a pinch of cream of tartar in a clean, dry bowl with an electric mixer until soft peaks form. Gradually pour in 1 1/2 cups superfine sugar, beating until the meringue is thick and glossy.

Caramel sauce

To make one quantity of caramel sauce, put 2 tablespoons unsalted butter, 1 1/4 cups light brown sugar, 2 teaspoons vanilla extract, and 3/4 cup whipping cream in a saucepan and cook, stirring, for 5 minutes or until the sauce has thickened.

Index

Photographers: Alan Benson, Cris Cordeiro, Craig Cranko, Joe Filshie, Jared Fowler, Ian Hofstetter, Chris L. Jones, Tony Lyons, Andre Martin, Luis Martin, Valerie Martin, Rob Reichenfeld, Brett Stevens

Food Stylists: Marie-Hélène Clauzon, Jane Collins, Sarah de Nardi, Georgina Dolling, Carolyn Fienberg, Mary Harris, Katy Holder, Cherise Koch, Michelle Noerianto, Sarah O'Brien, Sally Parker

Food Preparation: Alison Adams, Rekha Arnott, Ross Dobson, Michelle Earl, Justin Finlay, Jo Glynn, Sonia Grieg, Justine Johnson, Michelle Lawton, Valli Little, Ben Masters, Kerrie Mullins, Kate Murdoch, Briget Palmer, Kim Passenger, Justine Poole, Julie Ray, Christine Sheppard, Angela Tregonning

Laurel Glen Publishing
An imprint of the Advantage Publishers Group
5880 Oberlin Drive, San Diego, CA 92121-4794
www.laurelglenbooks.com

NOTE: Those who might be at risk from the effects of salmonella poisoning (the elderly, pregnant women, young children, and those with a compromised immune system) should consult their physician before trying recipes made with raw eggs.

Library of Congress Cataloging-in-Publication Data

Sweet food / [editors, Kim Rowney, Katharine Gasparini].
p.cm.
Includes index.
ISBN 1-59223-113-6
1.Confectionery. I. Rowney, Kim. II. Gasparini, Katharine

TX783 .S93 2003
641.8'6-dc21   2003048319

Printed by Tien Wah Press, Singapore
2 3 4 5 6   08 07 06 05 04

Editorial Director: Diana Hill
Editors: Kim Rowney, Katharine Gasparini, Gordana Trifunovic
Creative Director: Marylouise Brammer
Designer: Michelle Cutler
Photographers (chapter openers): Jared Fowler, Rob Reichenfeld
Stylists (chapter openers): Cherise Koch, Katy Holder
Picture Librarians: Anne Ferrier, Tom Pender
Chief Executive: Juliet Rogers
Publisher: Kay Scarlett

Front cover: Devil's food cake, page 91
Back cover: Lemon and passion fruit tarts with raspberries, page 333
Spine: Chocolate chip cookies, page 147